HYPNOTHI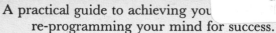

A practical guide to achieving you
re-programming your mind for success.

HYPNOTHINK

The Revolutionary Way to Re-programme Your Mind for Success

by

URSULA MARKHAM

THORSONS PUBLISHERS LIMITED
Wellingborough, Northamptonshire

First published February 1985
Second Impression August 1985

British Library Cataloguing in Publication Data

Markham, Ursula
  Hypnothink.
  1. Subconsciousness
  I. Title
  154   BF315

  ISBN 0-7225-0973-1

Printed in Great Britain by
Richard Clay (The Chaucer Press) Ltd,
Bungay, Suffolk

Contents

RON

My friend — my teacher — my love
This one's for you

Foreword

The sight was a chilling one. A scaffold dominated the stage. On a trapdoor, a rope around his neck, stood a man, his eyes closed in concentration.

Wires led from his chest to a surreal machine on one side. It uttered a regular 'beep' and a green light emanated from its monitor screen. It was an electrocardiograph used to measure the pulse of a human heart.

With every contraction of the heart muscle, a green tick travelled along the monitor line.

The capacity audience of 250 medical men, their wives and associates, were silent. Many of them, gripped by the tension of the moment, anxiously sat on the edge of their seats.

In the wings two doctors waited expectantly.

A hooded attendant, dressed as an executioner, stepped forward and pulled a lever. The trapdoor snapped open and the man fell through with sickening force. His body twitched as the sturdy rope jerked it to a halt.

The audience released a gasp of shock and fear. Simultaneously the electrocardiograph dramatically changed its pattern. The green heartbeat pulse on the screen flattened out. The moving tick — the sign of life — had gone. And the machine instantly set up its wail of warning — a high-pitched sustained note like a human scream. Its message — a heart had stopped beating!

The two doctors rushed out from the wings, reaching up to the figure dangling above. They each took hold of a wrist and searched fruitlessly for a pulse.

Through the loudspeakers a dispassionate voice counted off the seconds. Another attendant climbed up the scaffold and cut the rope.

The man slumped to the floor and his body was placed on a stretcher in full view of the audience. The electrocardiograph maintained its banshee wail. The off-stage voice continued to intone the passing seconds.

The man was Romark. The occasion was a unique demonstration that he could 'programme' himself hypnotically to stop his heart at will.

After four minutes Romark suddenly sat up. Slowly he revived. The machine began to record the signs of life again. Audibly the audience sighed with relief.

The experiment — staged in dramatic terms in order to draw the attention of the public — was an absolute success.

The two doctors who had checked Romark's heartbeat told the press later: 'We could find no trace of a pulse.'

Romark (real name Ronald Markham) had accomplished what many experts had regarded as impossible. By means of self-hypnosis he had demonstrated graphically that the human mind could control the human body to a literally death-defying degree.

And Romark had conducted his experiment not in front of credulous laymen, but before no fewer than 250 doctors, with two highly respected medical men actually testing his wrists for a pulse-beat.

That memorable experiment took place in the Lyric Theatre, Durban, in April 1972. I was there. I marvelled at the combination of showmanship and expertise which was revealed that night.

It was the showman in Romark which erected the scaffold on the stage and put the hangman's noose around his neck. Showmanship after all is the art of focusing attention.

But behind the showman a keen intellect was at work. Romark, as I discovered when I had the opportunity to meet him and talk with him, was a man of profound experience as a clinical hypnotherapist. For many years, in various parts of the world, he had been consulted by thousands of people seeking relief and help for all types of ailments and personal problems.

In many cases he had used his tremendous skill as a hypnotist as the key with which to unlock the doors to the hidden fears and phobias which are at the root of so many ailments.

His fame, both as a showman and a healer, spread swiftly. Romark stayed at the Durban Lyric Theatre for a remarkable 328 performances — thus becoming the holder of the Guinness Book of Records title for the longest-running one man show in world theatre history.

Off-stage he was even more in demand. Calls on his time for clinical work became so insistent and clamorous (many doctors were among those who personally sought his help) that he found it difficult to enjoy a moment's privacy.

Throughout this period of unremitting work and virtual round-the-clock activity, Romark continued to work to develop the psychological and philosophical theories which were the very heart of his success.

Every night on stage — and every day during his clinical work — he proved their validity.

When he hypnotized his assistant so that she could suspend her body between two chairs and support the weight of a 400 lb man sitting on her, the audience was duly dumbfounded.

They were astonished — as well they might be — when a volunteer from the audience came on stage and, at Romark's request, thrust a needle deep into the assistant's arm — and she neither felt pain nor bled. Under hypnosis her brain had suspended the laws of nature — or perhaps had demonstrated that there exist natural laws which orthodox medicine has no real knowledge of.

Equally, in private practice every day, Romark found that a virtually limitless number of apparently physical disorders disappeared 'magically' once the mental source of the trouble was revealed and emotionally recreated.

Man, Romark had discovered, was so very much a creature of the mind.

After his success in South Africa, Romark was booked by an American impresario for a visit to the United States.

There his success continued. His opening at the Huntingdon-Hartford Theatre in Los Angeles was greeted with unanimous enthusiasm by press and television critics. Stars and business celebrities sought his professional help. Shirley Jones was so ecstatic when Romark cured her of her life-long phobia about travelling that she threw a champagne party for him and publicly announced her gratitude.

Through it all Romark maintained his incredible pace of work. Instead of the normal number of performances — six a week — he gave fourteen a week. Every moment of his own time was devoted to interviews with the media and to private consultations.

Then he returned to Britain to fulfil commitments there.

As many a transatlantic air traveller knows, the shift from

America to Britain results in a time difference of eight hours which is deeply disorientating. Yet, without pausing to let his body adjust to the ensuing jet-lag, Romark plunged into a non-stop round of work on his BBC-TV series, clinical consultations and press and television interviews.

On 12 January 1974 Romark had a stroke . . .

A stroke often results in instant death. In many other cases the victim becomes a human vegetable — extensively paralysed. His powers of speech are severely impaired, various groups of muscles are rendered helpless, and sometimes permanent unconsciousness is caused.

Some people who have been felled by a stroke gradually regain some use of their paralysed limbs. With the aid of physiotherapy they slowly win back some of their former mental and physical prowess.

It is very rare indeed for someone who has suffered a major stroke to make a full recovery. Almost inevitably traces of the disaster will remain.

Romark was unconscious for three days and in bed in St Mary's Hospital, London, for six weeks. The Harley Street specialist who treated him told him: 'You will never be able to return to your previous way of life.' In other words — you will never work again!

Eight weeks to the day after having had the stroke, Romark was the guest star on a British television programme — Jimmy Saville's 'Clunk Click' show.

He conducted an experiment which required total concentration and intellectual control. It worked perfectly.

Twelve weeks after the stroke, Romark starred in his own show at the London Palladium. In the audience was the Harley Street specialist who had told Romark that he would never work again.

Romark had made a total — and incredibly swift — recovery. How?

How did Romark stop his heart for four minutes and then start it again with no after-effects?

How could he not only survive a massive and normally lethal stroke but also restore himself to full efficiency in a matter of weeks?

The answer lies in the technique of self-programming which Romark had developed as the culmination of his many years of research and experience as a psychologist, clinical hypnotherapist and showman extraordinary.

Romark called this system Hypnothink. It is hypnosis without a trance. It is a system of using your very own super-computer — your brain!

In the following pages you will learn how you can programme yourself by Hypnothink to achieve your legitimate aims, fulfil your personality and make the fullest possible use of your talents. You can be a successful human being in every way.

You are being offered the fruits of a lifetime of study, experimentation and wide-ranging experience in the belief that it can — and will — change your life immeasurably for the better.

ROY CHRISTIE

Anatomy of a Discovery

In most discoveries of profound importance there is one critical moment — a flash of recognition — an intuitive leap of the mind — which opens the door to a new perspective of thought.

Often it is something which has been in plain view, but which suddenly acquires a dazzling new significance.

Frequently the breakthrough comes as a logical development from years of painstaking experiment and apparently routine experience.

Sometimes a personal crisis provides an intensity of emotion which heightens perception.

ALL of these factors were present in the discovery of Hypnothink.

The following chapters recount, in chronological order, the events — over a period of twenty-six years — which resulted in the final formulation of the theory.

1.

How Hypnothink Began

In 1947 Romark — or plain Ronald Markham as he was in those days — came to London from his home in Newcastle-upon-Tyne to seek fame and fortune as an actor. He found no fame and no fortune — theatrical managements and agents seemed to have no particular regard for his qualities as an actor. In fact they were unanimous in their lack of enthusiasm about employing him.

He did have special qualities — but not as an actor — though he would only come to realize them later in life.

Young Ronald Markham, a man of impressive appearance and a melodious voice, acquired a bedsitter in Nottingham Place — an address distinguished by the fact that it is the next street to Harley Street where many eminent medical specialists have their consulting rooms.

Ronald had an apartment on the top floor. Living on the ground floor was the landlord — a psychiatrist who had recently come from Vienna to settle in Britain.

The psychiatrist was a strong believer in the usefulness of hypnotism in psychiatric therapy, but he was handicapped by the fact that his English was by no·means perfect and he spoke with an accent so heavily guttural that many of his patients had difficulty in understanding him. He was, however, resourceful enough to see in Ronald a useful ally.

So the future Romark found himself faced with a proposal which must be unique in the annals of therapy. The psychiatrist offered him free accommodation, in return for which Ronald would act as his 'parrot' and say the words in English which would induce sleep in his patients. As his lack of opportunity as an actor had made Ronald's income virtually non-existent, this was truly an 'offer he could not refuse'.

Romark recalls:

The psychiatrist knew what he wanted to say, but his heavy accent made him incomprehensible to most people. So he wrote down the phrases for me to learn, or slowly explained what he wanted to say, and I would hypnotize his patients on his behalf.

Because I couldn't find work as an actor, I went on doing this for a year. In that time I learned how to hypnotize people and I also acquired a grounding in practical psychology.

The psychiatrist worked on the generally accepted principle that it takes about twenty minutes to induce in people a sufficiently relaxed state for them to be hypnotized.

After a year of working as a 'parrot', I decided that my future as an actor was distinctly unpromising and I left London and returned to Newcastle. Naturally I spoke about my experience with my psychiatrist landlord and I would often use his method of hypnotism to help my personal circle of friends. I was successful in curing some of them of such ailments as asthma, migraine, psoriasis, and I also stopped many of them from smoking.

Word got around and in time I found myself running what amounted to a free clinic from my home. People would ask me for treatment and if I thought I could help I did. Sometimes they offered to pay me, but I always refused because I was not a professional psychologist. Nevertheless, I soon found that all my leisure time was being taken up with clinical work.

In 1967 I decided to become a hypnotherapist on a fully professional basis. I opened a clinic. My first receptionist was Coleen, a model who had come to me for help in losing weight. She had responded marvellously to hypnotism and had turned out to be a somnambule subject — someone who goes into a deep trance level without post-recollection.

Coleen became intrigued by the work I was doing and stayed on as a full-time helper.

Now I began to accept fees, although they were small, and soon we were inundated with work. I had a very high success rate with my patients and — of course — this is the best form of advertising.

I soon found that I was overloaded with cases. Time became of the essence. I simply could not devote twenty minutes to inducing the hypnotic state in each patient.

I tried an experiment. I told a patient that it would take only ten seconds to induce in him a hypnotic trance. I counted off the seconds and, on the count of ten, the patient was in fact hypnotized and I could proceed with his treatment.

To my initial surprise, I found that my patients went into precisely the same trance-state after ten seconds as that which they had only been reaching previously after twenty minutes of painstaking preparation.

I had made the important discovery that I could implant a suggestion while the patient was not hypnotized and, if he accepted it it would work.

In the course of his clinical work, it became clear to Romark that the depth of trance bore no relation to the efficacy of the treatment. Patients fell into three broad categories — they would go into light, medium or deep trance states. But the percentage of cures was constant.

At this time Romark was conducting a flourishing clinic. News of his successes had spread by word of mouth and he was simply inundated with patients.

Just then the British government instigated a propaganda campaign with the intention of bringing home to the public the dangers of cigarette smoking. Naturally this only served to intensify the flood of patients seeking Romark's help. So many people had already been cured of smoking by Romark's hypnotic techniques and the word had spread.

It would have been impossible for Romark to treat individually all those who wanted to stop smoking. It would have meant abandoning all his other patients — and even then there would not have been enough hours in the day.

To overcome this situation he hit on the idea of hiring the Newcastle City Hall and offering to cure, free of charge, any smoker who wished to attend a mass rally. A capacity crowd of 2,500 turned up on the appointed night. Television cameras were there to give the event national coverage.

At the end of the rally an astonishing 1,000 in that audience professed themselves to be cured of the habit! An in-depth analysis conducted one year later showed that 850 of those people had never again returned to smoking!

Romark was puzzled. Because of the circumstances under which the mass hypnotism rally took place, there were naturally widely

differing responses among the members of the audience. Some —
those who were naturally good hypnotic subjects — went into a
deep trance. Others went into a light trance and many were in a
medium state of trance. But some of those people merely closed
their eyes and listened to the suggestions which Romark had
implanted in their minds.

Even those members of the audience reported cures!

This led Romark to the irresistible conclusion that, just as the
depth of trance was irrelevant to a cure, the actual trance state itself
could be dispensed with.

For the next step in his voyage of discovery Romark left Britain.
He and his assistant, Coleen, had now developed a stage act which
was proving highly popular with cabaret audiences and they were
booked for a tour of South Africa.

When he arrived in Africa, Romark found that he was quite
unable to hypnotize any of the black Africans he met there. When
he tried to bring a black audience under the influence of hypnotism,
they merely smiled at him with happy unconcern.

This was worrying, to say the least. Nothing can be more
calculated to disturb a hypnotist than an absolute failure to hypnotize
his subjects. A partial failure was acceptable — but a total failure
was unheard of and flew in the face of generally accepted statistics
to the effect that a certain minimum percentage of human beings
are what is known as 'susceptibles' — that is, people who readily
accept hypnotism.

The more he thought about it, the more Romark was led to an
inevitable conclusion — these particular black people had never
seen hypnotism before, so they just didn't know how to react to
it. They didn't know what it was.

He decided to test his theory. He found a group of white people
who had seen and heard of hypnotism before and he hypnotized
these people in front of the black audience. From that point on those
black people were superb hypnotic subjects. They excelled the
'guinea pigs' they had seen in the degree and extent of their
susceptibility to hypnotism.

The whole point of that discovery boils down to one thing —
that the basis of hypnotism is imagination.

The black audience who had not been susceptible to hypnotism
in the first place had no starting point on which they could focus
their attention. Once that point of departure had been provided

for them, by the hypnotism of other subjects in front of them so that they could see for themselves what was involved in the process, it was possible for their own imaginations to take over.

Now it only remained for Coleen to provide one more crucial insight to focus Romark's attention upon the reality and validity of Hypnothink.

This came about at a later stage of the African tour. Every night on stage Romark would hypnotize Coleen. She would go into a deep-trance state and Romark would then suspend her body between two chairs and invite the biggest man in the audience to come on stage and sit on Coleen's stomach. In one demonstration — for the London *Daily Mirror* — a professional wrestler weighing 440 lb was photographed as he balanced his great weight on her slender 120 lb body — rendered as rigid as a steel bar by hypnosis.

At a later stage in the act, Romark would invite another volunteer from the audience to thrust a needle into Coleen's arm. There would be no sign of blood and Coleen would not feel or register any pain.

One night of the show Romark and Coleen were discussing, as they usually did, the events of the performance and the variety of people who had been onto the stage to be hypnotized. In the course of this discussion Coleen amazed Romark by telling him that she had not, in fact, been in a hypnotic trance during that night's performance. Suspecting a joke of some kind, Romark insisted that Coleen tell him of the conversations which had taken place during the routine with the needle (something which Coleen, as a somnambule, would not normally have heard). To his astonishment Coleen was able to repeat the dialogue exactly. She had, in fact, been conscious and unhypnotized during that night's performance.

When Romark questioned Coleen as to how she was able to support the weight of that gigantic man who had sat on her and how it was that she had not reacted to the needle in her arm, she merely shrugged her shoulders and told him that she did it 'because I always do'.

That single revelation by Coleen proved to be at the very heart of the development of Romark's theories. Some time later he was to expound upon his thinking:

I believe that, as human beings, we inherit certain genetic characteristics which affect our physical make-up, such as the colour of our eyes and our stamina.

But mentally we begin life like an empty computer. As we grow up, information is fed into the memory cells of that computer — our mind — and this gradually creates our personality and our character.

As we have all seen for ourselves, animals inherit certain instincts. When a sheepdog is still a puppy, for instance, it can be seen herding chickens together in a farmyard although it has never been taught to do so. It is a purely instinctive action.

In the same way, homing pigeons find their way back to their lofts, over distances of hundreds of miles and through the worst weather conditions, without ever having been taught to do so.

I believe that the first instinct which is firmly implanted in the human make-up is the inclination to succeed. People love to succeed — if it is an area which appeals to them.

In the early part of our life we receive an in-flow of information which creates certain patterns of behaviour — ways in which we react to certain situations.

But habit-patterns can be imposed on creatures in a planned way. This was demonstrated by the Russian scientist Pavlov with his experiments by which he caused dogs to salivate at the sound of a tinkling bell instead of when they received food.

In the same way it is possible for human beings to 'programme' themselves — just as a computer is programmed.

'Programming' is not as esoteric as it sounds. Practically all of us have programmed ourselves at some time or other to wake up early in the morning for an important appointment. A commonly used technique is to bang your head on the pillow the required number of times — seven times for seven o'clock in the morning, for example. A simple concept — but one which enables you to programme yourself for anything.

A research programme recently carried out at Stanford University in the United States has established that the mind is most receptive to this sort of suggestion programme at two periods in the day — just before waking in the morning and just before going to sleep at night.

It is not a feasible proposition for most of us to install complicated sleep-learning mechanisms for the early morning period of receptivity. Therefore we should make use of the period just before sleep.

The discovery that Coleen was performing remarkable feats on stage without being hypnotized was a remarkable breakthrough.

I have hypnotized thousands of people — on stage and off. Under clinical conditions I have proved over and over again that, if a person accepts the truth of a situation while under hypnosis, he will accept it when he is no longer under hypnosis.

An example is the case of a woman who came to me for treatment because she had a phobia about mice. She would have hysterics at the mere sight of one. Just the mention of the word 'mouse' was enough to unsettle her.

I hypnotized her and informed her that I was about to show a mouse to her. It would be the friendliest little creature she had ever seen. She would want to fondle it and pet it and it would be very affectionate towards her in return. Soon the subject was playing quite happily with the imaginary mouse. When I brought her out of hypnosis her fear of mice had disappeared. On the contrary, she was looking forward hopefully to actually seeing one.

The essence of this therapy is the fact that subjects in a hypnotic state trust the hypnotist implicitly. If they do not trust the hypnotist — they wake up. That is why, on stage, I can hypnotize a 400 lb man, tell him he is a ballet dancer, and he will deftly spin and twirl his way across the stage. He believes me when I tell him he is a ballet dancer — so he is one.

Coleen's experience provided the logical development from that established premise.

Perhaps I was perfunctory about hypnotizing Coleen on that night. But, whatever the reason, she failed to go into a trance. However, she had been performing these feats for months. She *knew* that she could do them. So, feeling no apprehension but exuding confidence, she blithely supported the weight of a heavy person and endured a needle stuck in her arm. The results were precisely as they would have been if she had been hypnotized.

Coleen proved that night that we do not really need hypnotism. All we need to do is to convince our own personal computer — our mind — that something is true. Coleen *knew* that when a member of the audience thrust a needle into her arm she would feel no pain and would not bleed from the wound. Her own computer — her mind — had been 'programmed' to this effect and it therefore produced the correct physical response. There was no sensation of pain. The wound did not bleed. Coleen had acquired an Inner Face, quite apart from hypnosis, which made it possible for her to do these things.

This discovery, on his very doorstep as it were, caused Romark to rethink his entire concept of the role of hypnosis in the treatment of ailments with a psychosomatic origin. As time went by, in fact, it resulted in him restructuring his whole attitude towards the 'cause-and-effect' relationship between the human brain and happenings in life. This subtle but crucial shift in mental perspective gave him the clue to Hypnothink.

Then, in one of those strange juxtapositions of events which often mark a breakthrough in human awareness, Romark reached a crisis point in his own life — a period of trial and suffering from which he emerged with the proof that Hypnothink works. He acquired that proof by staking his most valuable possession — his own health.

Romark, felled at the very pinnacle of success by a massive stroke, was forced to test his theory in hospital — using himself as the guinea pig.

2.
A Stroke Leads to 'Programming'

On 12 January 1974 Romark was sitting at his desk in his comfortable London flat. A few hours previously he had given a live radio interview in London. Since his return from the United States his days had been taken up with one interview after another with the press, radio and television. He was besieged with offers for concert tours, television appearances, suggestions for television series, requests for magazine interviews. They came from the United States, Britain and Africa.

Romark rose from his chair and took a couple of steps. His intention was to take a book from a bookcase. As he moved forward consciousness left him. A minute later Coleen walked into the room and found Romark sprawled across the carpet. When she was unable to revive him she sought medical help.

Romark was taken to the intensive care unit at St Mary's Hospital, London, where Dr Edward Orton, a consultant physician of Harley Street, was called in. He diagnosed a major stroke. His professional opinion was short and to the point: 'Romark will never work again.'

Specialists who examined the stricken patient said that his speech had been seriously impaired and he was extensively paralysed.

Romark's life-style was changed dramatically. Hour after hour, day after day, week after week, he lay in his bed, his normally active mind starved of material. The stimulating flow of patients with problems and show-business challenges had been cut off. He slipped into a mood of meditative tranquillity and self-appraisal.

For the first time in many years he had nothing to do but think — and plenty of time to do it in. He thought about the events which had led up to his illness and it came to him that every human being has the ability within himself to mould his future to a far more precise degree than is commonly imagined.

The human brain has mysterious powers — a fact which is accepted in the most respected medical and scientific quarters. In fact the threshold of the mind is regarded by many as the most exciting frontier which we have yet attempted to cross.

Romark had time to think of the significance of his experiences with hypnosis and suggestion — with the programming of the thought processes. He realized that success, once achieved, provided the springboard for further success. This led him to reflect on the procedure followed by trainers who prepare a promising boxer for future triumphs. In order to bolster the aspiring boxer's confidence they will often 'arrange' a victory for him. In the case of Primo Carnera, the giant Italian, his promoters 'bought' him victory over numerous opponents. But he went on to win the world title purely on his own ability.

At this point Romark reached the conclusion which lies at the very heart of Hypnothink. All those successes which are necessary to programme people for even greater things need only take place in the imagination.

It was a very basic need indeed which spurred Romark on to take a leap forward into this new landscape of the mind. It was his need to go to the toilet.

Let him tell it in his own words:

When I was in hospital after the stroke they wanted me to use a bedpan, but I didn't like the idea. I decided to use the toilet in the normal way.

But I was paralysed. I couldn't walk.

I decided to employ that theory which I had recently developed. I changed my self-image. To put it another way — I altered my Inner Face.

I knew for a fact that I was paralysed and that I couldn't walk. But I forced myself to *imagine* that I could walk as far as the toilet. I *pictured* myself walking as far as the toilet, and I *convinced* myself that I *had*, in fact, walked to the toilet.

I did this step by step — a laborious process. I didn't just imagine in general terms that I got up and went to the toilet. I pictured in my mind's eye every single detail — every move involved in the whole trip. And I expended on the thought process the same amount of time which would have been taken by the actual physical actions that I was visualizing.

I hadn't actually done it yet, so the action I contemplated — and which I saw so clearly in my mind — still lay in the future.

Finally I convinced myself — still within my imagination — that I had actually made the trip to the toilet and returned to my hospital bed.

At that point I got up out of bed, walked to the toilet and came back to bed once more without any conscious effort. The nurses, of course, were amazed.

I had succeeded in converting the future to the present tense. I had employed a form of hypnotism without resorting to the customary trance-state. I had been 'un-hypnotized' throughout.

If anyone reading these words thinks that a similar feat is beyond his capabilities, let me point out that the principle involved is precisely the same as the one by which countless people 'programme' themselves to wake up at the particular time in the morning without the help of an alarm clock.

Each person is capable of programming himself to achieve his aims.

I had had a stroke because of my own foolishness. My lifestyle was all wrong. I had been overworking for a long time — mainly because I was on an ego trip. In Durban I had broken the record for the longest-running one man show in world theatre history. That was an ego trip if ever there was one!

Breaking that record had been an extraordinarily difficult feat due to the sheer physical strain involved — 1,080 hours on stage. It was a one-man show. I was on stage uninterruptedly for every performance lasting over three hours — controlling as many as 100 hypnotic subjects simultaneously.

I had suffered from a heart condition since childhood and the specialists who examined me after the stroke established that, by subjecting myself to the strain involved in breaking the world record, I had weakened my heart still further.

Then, after leaving Africa, I had gone to the United States where I gave fourteen performances a week instead of the customary six.

I was doing too much in too short a time. My life-style had become so intense and high-pressured that it would inevitably have killed me.

These pressures are all too common in our modern society. The rat race is taking its toll to an ever-increasing degree. Human beings were never intended to live this way. That is why more and more people, particularly businessmen in high-pressure occupations, are having strokes and heart attacks.

A stroke is caused by a clot of blood detaching itself from the walls of the main artery, travelling to the brain and damaging cells there.

In a large percentage of cases this causes instant death. In many others the victim is extensively paralysed — even to the extent of becoming a 'human vegetable'. Some, through the use of extensive physiotherapy, make a partial recovery. It is very rare indeed for a serious stroke not to leave a visible and permanent trace in the victim.

Eight weeks to the day after having my stroke I was a guest star on Jimmy Saville's television show. I carried out an experiment which required a great deal of concentration on my part — and it was a complete success.

I did this with Hypnothink. It was just a continuation of that thought process by which I made myself walk to the toilet when I was paralysed.

Romark's own experience is the most dramatic possible example of the fact that Hypnothink works. But there are countless other examples. It would be useful to quote a few to demonstrate the range of human experience which can be affected.

While Romark was appearing in America in concert and on television, he became friendly with many stars. Scores of them consulted him privately for advice and help.

While in Hollywood he met Shirley Jones, then starring in the television series 'The Partridge Family'. Shirley is the stepmother of David Cassidy.

Romark recalls:

Shirley Jones and I had a mutual friend in California and he introduced us. One night she mentioned that an entire new series for television had just been written — and she was to be one of the stars. The concept was that the plot should take place on an ocean liner on its way to Acapulco.

We commented that it sounded like a marvellous idea and a pleasant setting for work. But Shirley said that when she read the first script she panicked. She said: 'It's impossible. I can't travel. I have a phobia about it.' She could see no possible way for the television company to get her on to a boat. She would have to turn the series down.

Shirley asked me if I could help her. I saw her the following day, gave her some advice on what she should do — and she was cured. Not only did Shirley Jones make that television series on the ship, but at the end of it she threw a party to thank me for making it possible.

What I had done was to help her to change her Inner Face. Instead of seeing herself as a human being who positively cringed from the prospect of travel, who thought of herself as insecure, unsafe and threatened aboard a ship, she now saw herself as a person radiantly happy at the prospect of a sea voyage — a woman enjoying everything an ocean trip had to offer.

She had programmed her own computer — her mind.

Shirley had been suffering from a phobic condition akin to agoraphobia, in which the victim becomes so afraid of venturing into the outside world that it is not uncommon to find him or her becoming a total recluse.

During the course of a 'clinic on the air' which I conducted on the radio from London, an elderly man 'phoned in to say that he was an agoraphobic. He described his symptoms. At one time he would be required, in the course of his profession, to address crowds of five or six hundred people. He was only able to do this if he knew that an exit from the hall had been prepared for him.

Agoraphobia is a common ailment. Hundreds of thousands of people, from all walks of life, are afflicted by it and it makes hermits of countless men and women. It becomes exceedingly difficult for them to find help because, after all, to seek help they have to leave their homes.

Before I discovered the mental technique which I have called Hypnothink, I would have treated Shirley Jones by hypnotizing her and searching for a possible cause of the phobia she had developed. It would have been necessary for her to re-enact the cause on a genuinely emotional level in order to purge herself of the effect.

With Hypnothink, however, Shirley was encouraged to re-programme her mental concept of herself — to change her Inner Face.

As the saying goes, it worked like a 'charm'. Only in this case the 'charm' she used was her own brain and the forces she called upon were the untapped powers of the human psyche.

I have identified Shirley Jones at her own express wish. She told me that she had benefited so much that she would appreciate her name being used in the hope that it might encourage other people to gain similar advantages.

Hypnothink proved beneficial to another well-known show business personality — a British cabaret artist. This artist, whom I shall call Susan, is a young woman of physical charm and strong personality. She is a singer and comedienne. And yet, in common with many other show business personalities, she was hounded by intense feelings of insecurity, inadequacy and lack of confidence.

These emotions would be at their most severe just before she went on stage to appear before an audience — in other words, at precisely the moment when she really needed to feel confident. The symptoms would become worse and her performance suffered as a result. We happened to meet socially and she showed a great deal of interest when I explained the principle of Hypnothink to her.

Some time later we met again and she told me that she had been using Hypnothink during an important engagement in London. The results had been spectacular. She had performed with exceptional confidence and poise and had been a great success with the audience.

Susan had thought of the future in the present tense — and had thereby succeeded in converting the future into the present. She had Hypnothought herself into a condition of confidence and success at a point in time before the actual performance which she had made her target.

When the time came, she went on stage and actually enacted the events she had previously Hypnothought in detail.

When Gary Player won the British Open Golf Championship in 1974, he was asked how he had achieved this feat — made all the more remarkable by the fact that he had frequently found himself in exceptional difficulties which would have shattered the confidence of a lesser player. The champion golfer told the press that he had developed a system of self-hypnosis which made him virtually invulnerable to tension. He went into a 'world of his own' where nothing could ruffle him.

It would seem that Gary Player has his own version of Hypnothink.

Hypnothink can enable overweight people to lose weight, people lacking in confidence to gain all the self-assurance they need, those who regard themselves as 'failures' to succeed in their ambitions, smokers to stop smoking — in fact, it can bring the wishes and dreams of each and every one of you to fruition.

3.

Inner Face

A vital part of Hypnothink is the initial self-assessment, followed by the process by which we change our Inner Face. In other words, we must first find out precisely what we really think of ourselves and then we must change that view of ourselves according to what we would like to be.

There is an old saying that you should 'look in the mirror and see yourself as others see you'. That saying is, of course, completely misleading because the one thing you do not see when you look in the mirror is yourself as others see you. You see yourself the wrong way round. Left is where right should be. Everything is in opposites. So, when you look in a mirror, you see your Mirror Face.

When other people look at you they see you from another perspective — they see your real Outer Face.

You also have your Inner Face — which is another way of describing your mind, your mental attitudes, the sum total of your personality and values, your individual characteristics as seen by you yourself. The trouble is that some people have an extremely distorted Inner Face. Romark tells of one such man:

This man came to see me because his head was 'too big'. He was convinced that he had the largest head in the world and that, wherever he went, people would laugh at him because of this.

Of course there was nothing especially odd or bizarre about the size of this man's head. In order to persuade him of this, I measured his head and then measured my own head in his presence. My head was bigger than his. This fact did not impress him at all. He was convinced that I had used a 'fake' tape measure.

I told him to go home, buy a tape measure and bring it with him to the next consultation. He did so and once again we measured heads. Naturally the result was the same as it had been on the first occasion

He was still unpersuaded — and he had an explanation for it.

He told me: 'You have a different type of body from mine, so that your head suits your body. But on *my* type of body I've got the biggest head in the world. I know that is the case because, when I walk along the street, I can see my reflection in the shop windows and it is quite obvious that my head is too big.'

No matter what I said and did, I could not dissuade this man from the view that he had an enormous head which everyone laughed at. His distorted Inner Face was fixed — rigid and unalterable.

We all carry around with us a picture in our minds of the sort of person we believe ourselves to be. This picture, or Inner Face, has been formed by our successes and our failures, our triumphs and our humiliations. Once this picture has been shaped, it becomes the basis for all our actions. It is the premise on which our entire personality is based.

All psychologists, and certainly all plastic surgeons, know from first-hand experience just how capricious and unpredictable people can be about their own concept of themselves.

For example a top model — we'll call her Annie — was told by a photographer that she had a perfect bust, a superb bottom, smashing legs and exceptional eyes. 'You would be absolutely perfect', he said, 'if it weren't for your nose. It's just a little too broad at the bridge.'

Those few words of perhaps flippant criticism became an obsession with Annie. Her friends and those who knew her well found it a harmless and slightly amusing personality foible of hers. One day she obtained a small role in a film and, as filming progressed, she became a very close friend of the Welsh actor who was the star. She told him about her wish to have the perfect nose. His generous reaction was to say, 'If you want the perfect nose, you shall have the perfect nose.' He took Annie to a leading plastic surgeon and she went into a nursing home to have an operation to alter the shape of her nose.

After the delicate operation had been performed, and as is always the case, she felt most uncomfortable. Her face was black and blue as though she had been mercilessly pounded by attackers.

Within a few weeks, however, the swelling and bruising had disappeared and Annie's new nose was there to be seen in all its theoretical perfection. It was the nose she had personally selected from the various shapes offered to her by the plastic surgeon.

Those who saw Annie with her new nose were, in fact, disappointed. Its beautiful symmetry had been destroyed. Its character had been removed.

But the change in Annie was remarkable. Her eyes blazed with vivacious confidence. She spoke with fire and eloquence. In her own eyes — in her Inner Face — she had become the ultimate beauty. Some of her bolder friends even told her that they preferred the shape of her nose as it had been before the operation, but she just laughed them off.

Annie had given herself an inferior nose on her outer face — but she had given herself an impeccable new Inner Face. She went on to become a happy and successful member of the international fashion set.

In precisely the same way, any plastic surgeon could cite countless examples of people who have had totally successful cosmetic operations which have not succeeded in terms of personality change. The 'ugly duckling' has been transformed physically, but still does not *feel* attractive.

The whole question of Inner Face can be very tricky. Romark recalls:

A young man came to me for treatment for psoriasis, which is a psychosomatic ailment, in my opinion, closely related to guilt feelings and self-punishment.

Psoriasis creates ugly suppurating sores which can afflict any part of the body. In the case of this young man, it affected his face. He had no success with girls and had become ashamed to go out in public.

With the aid of hypnosis I cured his psoriasis. But he still could not bring himself to go out with girls. He had used his psoriasis as an excuse for his natural shyness in approaching women. His Inner Face had nothing at all to do with his psoriasis.

Another common characteristic of people with a negative Inner Face is that they will act out their imagined inferiority and even wish to retain it. The man who says that he is an unsuccessful salesman will create circumstances which make it impossible to sell — even to a willing buyer. He is comfortable with his Inner Face as a poor salesman.

This is apparent too among many people who seek hypnotic aid in stopping smoking. Then they can say to their friends: 'I wanted to give up smoking so much that I even got myself hypnotized but it didn't help. I still smoke.' The truth is that those people do not really want to give up smoking at all. Something, perhaps the words of a doctor or a spouse or perhaps the pressures of propaganda emphasizing smoking's danger to health, has forced them to go through a charade of wanting to stop — and actually trying to.

There is plenty of self-deception with Inner Faces. That is why, if you want to benefit from Hypnothink it is essential that you evaluate yourself meticulously and try to see your true Inner Face.

Be very critical. Don't be kind to yourself.

Of course some people are so paranoid that they put all the blame for their faults onto others. Such people can never get a clear picture of themselves. They would need the help of a psychologist for accurate self-evaluation.

An important point to remember is that it is possible to change your Inner Face at any age. In fact, maturity of vision can be a distinct help.

What we are going to do is to hypnotize ourselves — but on a non-hypnotic level. We are going to change our Inner Face to the one we desire by using our imagination. We cannot achieve this by will-power. Will-power would actually have a distracting and negative effect.

We come into this world with minds which are like empty computers — virtually unprogrammed. Gradually we acquire certain patterns, such as those for survival — 'Don't put your finger on the hot stove,' for example.

In exactly the same way as these instincts were fed into our memory cells, we are going to put specific concepts into our minds. Once this information has been properly programmed, our mind — our own computer — will transmit it to our bodies as and when it is required.

The world is divided into two basic types of people — successes and failures. This even applies to physical health. Some people are constantly complaining about their health and are always rushing to consult their doctors. Others say: 'I'm never ill from one year to the next.' And they are not. They never have to see a doctor.

Some people say: 'It doesn't matter how much I eat, I never gain weight.' And it's true. There are people who even overeat to extremes and yet remain slim. There are those at the other extreme — those who say: 'I eat like a bird but I still get fat.' And when you check on these people and their eating habits, that statement turns out to be true.

Positive thinking works when it is consistent with a positive Inner Face. It cannot work if you have a non-successful Inner Face.

People who are successful have an in-built goal-striving mechanism. Their natural instinct is to reach for a target — and because they do so with confidence, they achieve it.

Hypnothink is an exciting concept because it deals in the future! We are all conditioned to think of the future as a nebulous abstract. The future, to most people, can be anything. It can bring disaster or it can bring happiness.

With Hypnothink we are going to think of the future in the present — and therefore we are using the future in the present tense in order to achieve our aims. In a way we are exploring the future and using it.

It is so important to realize that we learn to be successful by experiencing success. A person who has done nothing but fail knows nothing about success.

Years of experience in all aspects of clinical hypnotism bring the knowledge that there is no difference between actual experience and imagined experience. Imagined success can equal actual success.

You have already read the story of the woman who had the phobia about mice but who lost her fear once she had been persuaded under hypnosis that mice were friendly little creatures. Now Romark will tell you of another example of the efficacy of Hypnothink:

When I was in Los Angeles I was consulted by a man in his forties, a successful film producer and a man of considerable charm.

As soon as this man had entered his early forties his Inner Face had changed. He became persuaded that his sexual life was finished. Gradually he lost the capacity for sex. He became impotent.

I advised him that, before meeting his intended sexual partner, he should fantasize having successful sex with her. He should go through the motions, in every specific detail, in his mind — devoting to the imagined experience the same amount of time which would be occupied by him actually performing the act.

Once again we applied the principle that, once you score a success, you can repeat it. In the case of this particular man, he Hypnothought a successful sexual encounter with his chosen partner. Then, in reality, he merely had to repeat his earlier success.

He found that he was capable of enjoying a vigorous sex life once more.

He had proved to his own dramatic satisfaction that an imagined experience can be equivalent to the actual experience.

He had altered his Inner Face quickly and successfully.

Our next step is to explore the uses of imagination and apply it to the process of programming yourself in order to alter your own Inner Face.

4.

Imagine a Happy Ending

The uses of imagination are many. But the faculty of the imagination is much abused by neglect in our modern society. Television and other forms of mass media have become substitutes for the flights of fancy once indulged in by man.

Imagination is the essence of Hypnothink. How can we harness our imagination to gain positive and beneficial results?

Intense imagination feeds a set of facts into the brain. Then, when a future situation occurs, the personality reacts accordingly.

It is strange that, even at this stage of our development, when we pride ourselves on our technological knowledge, so little is really known about how the brain works. Scientists can explain the cell structure, but they cannot say what process initiates concepts or thoughts.

That is the essential difference between a computer and a human brain. A computer cannot initiate a concept. It simply does what it is told to do — although it does it efficiently.

A human brain — even the most lowly — initiates thoughts constantly — many of a sublime nature.

With Hypnothink, we combine the qualities of the brain with the qualities of the computer. Your mind conceives the idea of programming yourself for the future and your brain receives the factual input.

The quality of our imagination varies — just as people vary. Poets and writers have to have a fertile, active imagination. Their output depends on it. People in other, more mundane, occupations allow their imaginations to become lazy. It is like a muscle which has fallen into disuse and has atrophied. But virtually everyone has at some time used this muscle — this faculty of imagination. Unwittingly we have all tinkered with Hypnothink.

Who among you has not pictured an event with extraordinary

vividness — only to find it coming true at a later stage?

Imagination is one of the qualities which separates man from animals. Animals work purely on instinct. We have our own set of instincts, but in addition we have been blessed with imagination. The principles of Hypnothink will surely 'click' in your mind because they will activate your memory cell mechanism. This will 'ring a bell'.

The trouble is that most of us use our imagination and our brain erratically. We do our jobs, we look at television, we read a book or a magazine. The vast majority of us are not living up to our full potential.

We have a need for emotional satisfaction. We need to explore new territories of the mind and the imagination — to cross new horizons. We need a fuller life.

By changing our Inner Face we can achieve these objectives. So we need to know how to programme our Inner Face. Romark tells of his own early 'programming'.

When I look back on my life, I realize that I started programming myself when I was still a child.

My first attempt at adjustment of the future took place when I was a small boy. My father at that time would travel away from home on business from Monday to Friday.

If I had been naughty during the week, my mother would say to me: 'Just wait until your father gets home and I tell him what you have done.' I would live through the rest of that week in a state of terror because I was mortally afraid of my father. I didn't want him to be told about my misdemeanours, trivial though they were, because I knew that he would fly into one of his terrible rages.

So I used to think to myself, very positively, that my father would not return on the Friday. He would only get back on the Saturday. Strangely, more often than not, I was able to go to sleep peacefully on the Friday night because my father had been delayed by a puncture, car trouble of some sort, or a business crisis.

Perhaps it was mere coincidence. But perhaps that small child, lying terrified in his room and imagining with vivid intensity, was affecting life outside that room in an astonishing way.

When I was older, about thirteen, I was evacuated to a boarding school at Penrith in Cumberland. This was during the Second World War when the Germans were bombing the principal British cities.

At the hostel where I was staying there was a master called Mr Thorn who was something of a sadist. He would keep a tally of our misdemeanours during the day and then give us a caning at night.

If you are wearing very thin pyjamas and have to bend over to receive whacks, a caning can be really painful. So I used to persuade myself, whenever I knew that a caning was due, that it was already over and I had felt no pain whatsoever. As a result, I never *did* feel any pain.

Gradually, as the years passed and my experience increased I developed my theory up to the point where I could bring about an actual change in my state of physical well-being — as in the case of overcoming the paralysis brought on by my stroke.

In order to be as receptive as possible to the process of programming, it is important that you induce a state of happiness and cultivate an attitude of sincerity and decisiveness.

The process is not unlike evoking a film of the desired events on the screen of your own mind. But remember that you must always have a happy ending. The process of Hypnothink must always be a pleasurable one. Don't allow an atmosphere of boredom or repetitive dullness to creep in. Make your Hypnothink exciting, stimulating and rewarding. You should look forward with keen anticipation to your sessions of Hypnothink.

For many people their problems are manifold. They don't simply have one problem which they wish to overcome. They might have many, some of which may overlap.

The procedure to follow is to take one problem at a time, visualize and imagine the solution to it and slowly feed it into the computer of your mind.

But before going on to the mechanics of programming, let us discuss the mental state which you should achieve before you even begin.

The strange thing about being happy is that so many people feel guilty about it. No one should ever feel guilty about being happy. Happiness equals health. It is a long-established fact that, when you are happy, your organs function more efficiently. There is an old saying, attributed to King Solomon: 'A merry heart doth good but a broken spirit drieth up the bones.' The Bible, in both Old and New Testaments, prescribes joy and rejoicing as a means to righteousness.

We know from modern sociological studies that unhappiness and unhappy environments — such as broken and disunited homes — can breed crime.

Many people have a back-to-front philosophy. 'If only I were successful I would be happy.' They should reverse this line of thought. Be happy and *then* you will be successful.

Spinoza said: 'Happiness is virtue, not the reward of virtue.' And in his *Ethics* he added: 'Because we delight we can restrain our lusts.'

Literature abounds with sayings which make this point: *happiness creates health.*

When people are gloomy and depressed their friends say to them: 'Why don't you look on the bright side?.' Unhappiness doesn't solve any problems at all. It merely creates new ones.

Happiness should not be dependent on distant hopes. People who think: 'When I pay my debts I'll be happy' or 'When I'm married I'll be happy' or 'When I have a baby I'll be happy' are putting their happiness into the future and making it conditional on something else.

So many people also acquire the bad habit of reacting according to an established behaviour pattern when things go wrong. For example, they think: 'I've lost my money so I must be unhappy.' Or: 'I have done something wrong, so no one will respect me.' Or: 'This has upset me, so I must be angry.' The truth is that you don't *have* to do any of these things. There is no compulsion upon you.

Robert Louis Stevenson said: 'Being happy enables you to be free from domination by the outside world.'

Don't make the mistake of allowing outside opinions to alter your own assessment of events.

Take the case of a woman whose unmarried daughter has a baby. The woman may think: 'What will people say? How can we bear the disgrace?' But let us separate fact from opinion. The daughter is unmarried — that's a fact. She has an illegitimate child — that's a fact. But the rest is pure opinion and speculation.

The word 'habit' has two meanings. It can mean behaviour and it can mean clothes. Our behaviour fits us and our clothing fits us. If we have bad habits, it is rather like wearing badly fitting clothes. If we develop new habits, it is like putting on new clothes. And the more those new habits become a part of us, the better those new clothes will fit.

You have to acquire the habit of telling yourself that whatever you are doing, success is a certainty. Say to yourself: 'I will practise every day acting the part of the new person I wish to be. There is absolutely nothing to stop me from being happy. I will not allow myself to be pessimistic.

These are rules of living. Stick to them.

Many people are unable to live with themselves when life or circumstances thrust new habits upon them. The winners of football pools, for instance, include an inordinate number of people who later attempt suicide at some stage. And yet, ironically, these same people have spent a large part of their lives thinking: 'If only I could win the football pools, everything would be all right and I would be happy.' When they do win, what happens? As often as not, their world comes apart and they suffer what is known as a nervous breakdown or a crisis of self identity. They think: 'I have acquired a lot of money. That means I shall now have to play a role in life quite different from the one I have been playing.'

That, of course, is the opposite of the programming process of Hypnothink.

These unfortunate 'winners' try to play the part of someone they are not, instead of programming their Inner Face to create a new person within themselves.

Because they have adopted the role or the habits of someone they are not, the habits do not fit but cause friction, discomfort and feelings of inferiority and unhappiness.

They torment themselves with thoughts like: 'I can't associate with monied people . . . I don't look like one of them.' They cease to think in terms of what life holds for them to look forward to and start to think in terms of what is expected of them. They become aimless — life has lost its purpose, its goal.

One must always have something to look forward to. Don't waste time looking back repeatedly on past errors. Look forward with pleasure to the goals you hope to achieve If you don't strive, you don't live.

How many men retire from active work and then die? And how many tycoons carry on a highly active work schedule and live well beyond what is considered normal retirement age?

It is a trait of human nature that we do not like to admit our mistakes to ourselves. So we misinform ourselves. Yet truth is essential; communication with ourselves is vital

Huge businesses have been known to fail because tyrannical tycoons would not listen to bad news. If a member of the staff said that an aspect of the firm was doing badly, he would be reprimanded or merely banished from the great man's presence. As a natural result no one would be the bearer of bad news or criticism. So the centre of the vast operation — the tycoon himself — would never receive the information which would have enabled him perhaps to rectify faults and even save a whole structure from disaster.

Adolf Hitler was just such a man. Every time a general brought him bad news, he would be demoted or banished. That was one of the reasons for the disarray of the German military machine in the latter stages of the war.

A flow of accurate information is absolutely essential.

Look in the dictionary. The word 'sincerity' is defined as: 'Clean, pure, being in reality what it is in appearance'. Sincerity in human personality is derived from a combination of self-understanding and honesty. Assess yourself with honesty — and yet with sympathetic understanding.

Decisiveness plays an important part in a successful personality. Don't dither. Decide on a course of action and follow it right away. People who delay decisions by procrastinating put themselves in a situation where they have added the element of time to whichever problem confronts them. But they have not gained any certainty. The fact that you delay the start of something doesn't mean that the project must succeed. It can still go wrong. Of course, if you have made a wrong decision, your plans can still go awry even if you start it right away. The point is, however, that time itself cannot increase the odds in your favour. It is better to make the occasional mistake through taking action than to live in the nothingness of a state of permanent stalemate.

One instinct common to most of humanity is the love of gambling. It is those people who do not ever gamble on themselves or their future who seem to develop gambling fever in casinos or on racetracks. They have always forced themselves to live a life of caution and security, so that their natural instinct for gambling has been suppressed. It is just such people who will one day 'have a flutter' and soon find themselves addicted to it.

Why not gamble on yourself and your future? Have enough confidence in yourself to test your abilities to the fullest degree

You can easily practise self-improvement on minor issues.

Ordinary living on a day-to-day basis takes quite some doing. Every day is full of petty challenges and problems. Start by adjusting your programme of self-improvement in ordinary living.

An important fact to bear in mind is that, in order to be a successful personality — and to believe in yourself as one — other people's feelings have to be considered. The more you can make other people feel important and esteemed, the more important *you* will be to *them*.

Carlyle once said: 'The most fearful unbelief is unbelief in yourself.'

Whenever someone says to you, 'I can't do it,' you know that that person has lost the game of life. There is no virtue in being excessively humble and self-denegrating.

Self-doubt lies at the heart of all jealousy. Never dramatize yourself as an object of pity. Never say: 'I feel sorry for myself.' And don't ever be afraid of appreciating your own virtues. Pride in your own worth only becomes egotism if you assume that you created yourself and should therefore take the credit for the creation.

Confidence in oneself is built up by the experience of success — whether that success is real or strongly imagined. Therefore, when you are conjuring up your mental image of yourself, be sure that you remember past successes — however minor — and concentrate on those. Forget the failures which come to us all from time to time.

Too many people dwell on their failures and constantly remember them. This is the surest way to destroy any remaining vestiges of self-confidence. One remembered success can obliterate the effect of hundreds of failures. So forget the failures and let the successes reinforce each other. At the same time, don't live a lie, pretending to be someone you are not. You are still you, but a more successful — and therefore more confident — you.

The self image you create for yourself must be compatible with you. You cannot change the intrinsic *you* in the sense of transforming yourself into a different person altogether. But you can certainly discover far more about yourself that you can truly admire and you can rid yourself of those failings which are not so admirable.

If you make a mistake, that does not mean that you as a person are no good. It simply means that you made a mistake — which you won't necessarily make again. If you make an honest assessment of yourself you are bound to find imperfections. Learn to tolerate these rather than to blame or over-criticize yourself for them. After all, no one is perfect.

You are no more rendered worthless because you have made a mistake — however big that mistake might be — than a Wimbledon tennis champion is made worthless by serving a double fault. An opera star who sings one duff note is not banished from the world of music. These are the kind of thoughts and principles which can help to induce the right frame of mind for the process of self-programming.

On a purely physical level it will probably help you if you can relax completely — reproducing, in fact, the pleasant state of muscular relaxation which is an essential characteristic of the hypnotic state. To do this, just follow this basic routine:

Think of your body as being as heavy as lead. Start with your feet — they are heavy — feel the weight of them. Then work your way up your body, to your legs, your torso, your arms and hands — feel the heaviness of each part of you in turn. Concentrate particularly on your neck, jaw, shoulders and head — this is where the effects of tension are usually most obvious — let them become so heavy that they need to sink back into the chair or bed you are on. Finally, breathe deeply, being very conscious of the sound and rhythm of your breathing. At this stage, if you ask a friend to lift up your arm and let it go, it should fall like a stone, with no resistance at all. If this is the case, you are completely relaxed.

The next step is to set a target for yourself in your mind. You can make your target anything in the entire area of human endeavour. The vital part of this process is the visualization of the problem or of the situation in which you wish to see yourself functioning efficiently.

When you present your brain with a problem, it automatically scans its memory banks for relevant information to enable it to cope with the situation. It has to recognize the problem before it can respond to it.

An inventor has a great problem if he has to invent something utterly new. To illustrate this point — it was comparatively easy to invent television because radio had already been invented. So it was known precisely what was required — radio with pictures.

One of the most famous quotations of all time says: 'If the human mind can *conceive* of something, the human mind can *achieve* it.' You don't need to know how to build a car, or how it works, in order to drive one. Nor do you need to understand the mechanism of a typewriter in order to learn to type. In the same way, you don't need to know how the human brain works in order to use it.

When you apply Hypnothink there is no need to worry about making mistakes because those mistakes actually play an important role in the whole process. (This will be discussed in greater detail later in Chapter 5.)

For the purposes of an example, let us assume that your first target will be a speech which you are expected to deliver before an important audience in a few days time. You will be expected to talk for thirty minutes on a subject familiar to you. Very often it is the fear of the initial response from the audience which saps the confidence of people unaccustomed to public speaking. They anticipate an attitude of rejection or hostility from the audience, so, from the moment they appear before that audience, their own attitude is wrongly influenced. This, in turn, creates in the audience the very attitude the speaker feared in the first place.

Having prepared your mental attitude, as we discussed earlier in this chapter, as well as your physical attitude (by complete relaxation) you are now ready to imprint upon your brain, by the process of vivid imagination, the actual delivery of your speech.

On the television screen of your own mind allow the event to unfold exactly as you would wish it to happen. You are seated at the main table, calm and fully in control of your emotions. You are introduced as the next speaker; you rise, smiling, and assume your position in front of the microphone. You go through your speech word by word. At the appropriate moment, your audience provides you with the response you desire. They laugh at an amusing line, respond with gravity to a more serious point of discussion. Perhaps at the end of the speech you answer a few questions from the audience before resuming your seat.

Here are a few points to bear in mind:

1. You are expected to deliver a speech lasting thirty minutes. Therefore in your programming you must occupy thirty minutes of elapsed time.
2. Repeat the programming process each night just before falling asleep.
3. Be specific in your programming. It is of absolutely no use to think in general conceptual terms, such as: 'I'm going to go out there and captivate them! I'm going to be great!' That is

meaningless and useless. See every detail in your mind's eye — clearly and vividly.

4. Don't conceive of the possibility of error. There is no need to take into account the possibility that you might stumble over a word. Your brain will automatically take care of such eventualities.

5. During the programming, visualize your speech-making in terms of pictures. The brain retains pictures much more readily than it does words. Don't give yourself a comforting verbal account in your mind of what you will do. Actually see yourself delivering the speech — complete with hand gestures, facial attitudes, smiles and frowns.

6. *Remember that will-power does not enter into this process at all. Imagination is the key.*

7. There is no short-cut to success. Programming yourself in delivering such a speech does not mean that you do not have to memorize your speech. Obviously you must be word-perfect, otherwise you will not have fed all the vital information into your computer — your brain.

To sum up: you have induced in yourself a harmonious attitude of mind. You have memorized your speech thoroughly. You picture yourself delivering it, word by word, occupying just as much time in your 'daydream' of it as you would in actually uttering it, and you have brought the entire episode to life in your imagination with vivid effect.

After this, you will find that, when you finally come to deliver your speech to a live audience, actual experience will imitate the imagined experience. It might be described as another example of life imitating art.

You will have been well prepared and thoroughly programmed for the speech. The result will be a successful occasion for everyone concerned. And, as the following chapter will explain in greater detail, any mistakes you might make — any errors — will only serve to focus you even more precisely on your target.

5.

Errors Can Help You

We live in a technological age. Men have walked on the moon. Missiles can bridge the continents. Computers are harnessed for such disparate tasks as compiling telephone bills and shooting down hostile aircraft. It is fitting, therefore, that Hypnothink should make use of a missile-age principle in its application to human aspirations, no matter how significant or subjective they may be.

What happens when a missile is launched at a moving target? The situation is one of constant flux. As the missile proceeds towards its target area, it transmits back to its controlling computer information about its position — and its position in relation to the target. The target, meanwhile, keeps moving. The missile reaches the point at which it was originally aimed. The target is no longer there. The missile feeds back the information that it has missed — and the computer redirects it to the new position of the target.

In other words, the process is one of continuing error, subsequently corrected, until finally the missile reaches its target. That process is known in technological jargon as 'negative feed-back'.

In Hypnothink precisely the same principle will come into play in your brain.

Let us suppose, for example, that you are overweight and have decided to Hypnothink yourself slim. You have changed your self-image from fat to slim. You have seen yourself in fine clothes which fit you well, flattering your slim outline. You will have pictured yourself enjoying only those foods calculated to help you lose weight slowly and consistently until you have reached your target weight. You have imprinted a vivid picture upon your brain.

So, on the second day of your get-slim programme, you are offered a slice of cake by a friend. You pick it up and munch away. Three-quarters of the way through the cake you remember with a start that you should not be eating it. Your programmed brain receives the negative feed-back: 'This is *not* the right thing to eat in terms of the target desired.' In future you will either refrain from eating cake again or, equally likely, you will develop an instinctive dislike for cake — until your target has been achieved and your weight has been stabilized at the desired level.

The point to remember is that, once you have programmed yourself, you no longer have to make a conscious effort not to eat certain types of food. Your 'computer' just won't allow you to eat the wrong things.

Romark tells of an actual example of this truth:

A journalist called Ian Gray approached me in Durban, South Africa. and asked me if I would undertake a public experiment with him. He wanted to lose sixty pounds in weight, using my hypnotic techniques, and he would give a full account of his progress in his column in the *Sunday Tribune*.

Mr Gray lost weight exactly as specified in the treatment — at the rate of one pound per day.

And what is more, as he reported in his column, his programming was so effective that he could not stray from the patterns of correct eating even when he wanted to.

As he reported, no specific foods had been forbidden to him. But he had been programmed to the effect that he would know what he should eat and what he should not eat. Halfway through his slimming campaign his wife presented him with a plate of steak and chips. Ian, his wife and their table guests were in the midst of conversation and, unthinkingly, Ian picked up a fork to spear a mouthful of chips.

As he stabbed at the chips, the fork inexplicably missed, sending the chips flying across the table. Everyone stopped talking and looked at Ian Gray and the chips. He tried again. Once more he found that he could not spear the chips with the fork.

Then he realized — as he reported in his column to his readers — that his mind was resisting his attempt to eat food which was contrary to his programmed requirements.

Ian Gray lost the requisite amount of weight — and his weight has remained constant ever since.

Each and every time you move into the path of error, an alarm bell will ring in your brain. The effect of this is to nudge you back on course again, until you finally reach your target.

A good analogy is that of an aircraft landing in a thick fog. The pilot cannot see a thing, so it is no use him relying upon his own vision. He has to make use of radar.

If the pilot is making a perfect landing the radar won't give him any indication at all. But, as soon as he wanders off course, the radar system will alert him to that fact and he will make the necessary correction. His errors actually ensure the accuracy of his landing.

It is likely that one of the first people to think of this theory of negative feed-back was the man who invented the practice swing in golf.

Nearly all golfers take a practice swing before they take an actual swing at the ball. With many of them it doesn't make the slightest difference — they play a duff shot anyway.

But many years ago there was a golfer with a theory not unlike Hypnothink. He did more than simply take a practice swing; he strongly imagined that he was hitting the ball, connecting with just the right amount of velocity and precisely the right torque. He 'saw' the ball hurtling through the air and watched it land on the green. As he took his practice swing he saw all these events brightly and clearly in his mind's eye. Then he stepped up to the ball and took an actual swing with his club.

At that moment his memory cells, programmed by his own vivid pre-vision, created precisely the muscular effort which was required to match his mental conception of the event. He duplicated, in fact, what he had previously conceived in his imagination.

From that moment onward that golfer's game improved dramatically. Of course, he naturally kept up the procedure of having a practice 'think' before actually playing the ball. His friends, observing his actions and seeing the improvement in the quality of his golf — and yet having no idea of what was going on in his mind — put it all down to that practice swing. So they began to emulate him. And that is why all golfers take practice swings!

As Romark explains, Hypnothink is quite surprisingly effective in its application to sports.

The validity of Hypnothink in relation to sport was demonstrated publicly when I made an appearance on Southern Television in Britain.

My interviewer was Barry Westwood and he made it clear that he was extremely sceptical about Hypnothink. He was distinctly non-cooperative and said in a forthright fashion that he did not believe in hypnotism.

We decided to carry out an experiment in Hypnothink in front of the camera.

We placed a matchbox on the carpet, fifteen feet from Barry who was holding a golf putter. I put him through the Hypnothink procedure of imagining that he was successfully striking the ball so that it would hit the matchbox on the carpet. He duly visualized the full details of this process, the swing of the club, its contact with the ball, the exact flight of the ball and its final contact with the matchbox.

I then asked him to turn his back and Hypnothink the process once more. After he had done this, Barry put his imagined feat into reality. The result was absolute success. At my request Barry hit the ball repeatedly — no fewer than seven times. Each time he succeeded in striking the matchbox.

Then Barry turned to the camera and told his viewing public that he was now deliberately going to miss the matchbox. He struck the ball and, just as it had done previously, it hit the matchbox. Barry Westwood had been so well programmed that he could not deviate from his pattern of success.

Let us now take negative feed-back a stage further.

Think of what happens in a cricket match. A batsman hits the ball and it flies to the boundary. A fielder decides to intercept it. He runs to catch it — and this apparently simple action means that his brain has to work out where the ball will fall, the speed at which the ball is travelling, the decrease of its velocity, the probable increase or decrease in the speed of running required to meet the ball at precisely the right moment, control the mechanism of the hands so that the fingers close at exactly the right moment to pluck the speeding cricket ball from its flight path.

That is missile technology — negative feed-back. But the human brain does it all instinctively. The fielder doesn't think consciously of all those things which have to be done — he simply does them. His brain sends messages to the muscles which propel his body in exactly the same way as the computer sends instructions to one of the missiles under its control.

Many people have a hazy sort of awareness of this process and of the efficacy of Hypnothink within their own lives. Sometimes people will convert this semi-subliminal awareness into superstition or ritual.

A tennis player, for example, will often throw a ball a certain height into the air in the belief that, if he doesn't, he will be unlucky. What he is really doing is reproducing an occasion when he threw the ball in just that manner and he served the best service of his life. His brain is trying to reproduce the experience of success.

One player who did precisely this during the 1974 championships at Wimbledon was Jimmy Connors, who went on to become champion.

Connors' procedure was to place one ball in his pocket in case of a fault and bounce the other three times before throwing it in the air for the service. He never departed from this ritual. Once he was distracted by a ball-boy as he was going through that ritual bouncing. Connors stopped and began the whole ritual all over again — three bounces, throw the ball in the air, serve. He believed that if, for some reason or other, he had been prevented from bouncing the ball three times, his playing pattern would have been so disrupted that he would have been eliminated from that year's competition at Wimbledon.

It is important to remember that you must not try consciously to make this process work. The brain will function quite automatically.

For example, if we move suddenly into a cold temperature, our body informs us automatically. It tells us when we are hot or when we are frightened. The human brain has clocks and meters which science does not begin to understand.

Romark tells of an example of the accuracy of these 'brain clocks':

When I had my clinic in Newcastle-upon-Tyne, I was consulted by an extremely obese woman. (This case history is discussed at greater length in my book, *The Sins of the Fathers*.) I placed the lady under hypnosis and implanted the suggestion that she would lose one pound a day for a predetermined period. She proved to be an ideal patient and the weight simply fell away from her at the rate of precisely one pound a day.

Then one day she arrived at my consulting rooms in a state of some distress. She apologized profusely, saying that she didn't know what had come over her, but she had just been on an eating binge. She had consumed an entire loaf of bread and butter with jam. She must have put on so much weight.

I put my patient on the scales — and she had lost precisely one pound for each day that had passed since the last time I saw her.

What had happened was that the clock in her brain had told her that she had lost *too much* weight in the prescribed time and had compelled her to eat furiously in order to *put on* enough weight to meet the precise requirements.

That, of course, was before I discovered the astonishing efficacy of Hypnothink — hypnotic effects without hypnotism.

In London I was consulted by a leading woman publicist who told me that she suffered from what she described as 'chocolate-itis'. She couldn't resist chocolates.

I suggested that she imagine as strongly as she could that every time she ate a chocolate she would feel nauseous. I said that she should Hypnothink this state of affairs.

The next day this patient told me that she had not had a chocolate all day and that the system had worked with 'upsetting' efficiency. Upsetting because, with human perversity, she somehow missed the enjoyment of the chocolates. But her rapid weight loss soon cheered her up.

In order to dramatize the principles of Hypnothink we have drawn comparisons with computers and missiles. But other pieces of equipment are given negative indicators on a visual level. Think of the common household iron, for instance. It can come equipped with a red light to indicate when it is overheating. In using this sort of equipment, a person is aware of the negative indicators — but not to an overriding extent. This awareness does not hinder us in the task we have set our mind to — such as ironing the sheets.

The same attitude should apply in the use of the Hypnothink process. We must 'glance' at our negative indications without becoming obsessed by them.

If a golfer knows that there is a sand-trap in his path, it is enough for him to have that knowledge. If he *concentrates* excessively on the trap, he is quite likely to put the ball right into it. His target is the green and he is *aware* of the existence of hazards.

When we programme ourselves for success we substitute positives for negatives. We let our brain guide us out of danger. If you have programmed yourself well, your brain will steer you away from trouble and on to the path of success with the aid of automatic reflex and negative feed-back.

6.

The Thought is Father to the Deed

One doesn't have to go so very far back into the history of medicine to reach the days when a general practitioner was armed against the ills which beset mankind with only two basic weapons — a grey medicine and a pink one.

The grey medicine was rather sour and was for adults. The pink one was sweetish and was for children.

A patient needed a lot of faith in those days because that was usually what determined whether or not he pulled through. If the patient believed in the doctor, the medicine tended to work. If not, it did not.

Faith heals.

Hypnothink represents a breakthrough on a subject which has intrigued and yet eluded scientific thought since the beginning of time — the relationship between mind and body in the complex interaction which makes up the human being.

Faith in oneself — a positive, strong, radiant Inner Face — is the unshakeable foundation upon which success and personality are erected. Romark draws an example from life:

Two tennis players I knew were matched in France. Player A won six-nothing three times in a row. A few weeks later the players were drawn to play each other once more, this time in Britain. Player B approached the match at a tremendous disadvantage. He had a memory pattern of stupendous defeat after the thrashing inflicted upon him in France.

The other player, by contrast, had an Inner Face of resounding success to buoy up his confidence and programme him for yet another success.

By utilizing the principles of Hypnothink, player B programmed himself into an attitude of success and, after a ding-dong match, he just managed to beat player A. Normally it would have been a rout, a non-contest. But through the adjustment of Hypnothink, two fine players met on equal terms and the truly better player won.

Success does not have to be real. It can be imagined. The effect is just the same.

These same principles can be applied to all sports and to every walk of life.

If a boxer in training is taught to regard a punch-bag as a live opponent, and to make a point of knocking him out, the boxer will be programming himself towards success. When he does meet the other fighter in the ring, his brain will help him achieve the necessary physical responses to obtain that result in reality.

Hypnothink is just as applicable in a totally different field of activity. A scholar, for instance, might wish to improve his learning capacity in preparation for a particularly taxing examination. Following the principles of Hypnothink, he will visualize himself at the examination desk, reading the questions and writing out his answers. The questions posed will be within the ambit of his capacity and he will be able to answer them easily within the time allotted.

(Of course the scholar must have done his swotting. There is no miraculous process by which a mind can absorb information without studying it.)

But by intense programming the scholar's brain will help him to 'spot' the right questions, so that he will be more than adequately prepared.

This process also eliminates such fringe handicaps to the examination procedure as excessive anxiety. It will also eliminate the arch-enemy of any student — the negative activity of reading without thinking, without absorbing any of the material scanned by the eye. With the proper use of Hypnothink the scholar will find learning an enjoyable and constructive action in which knowledge is retained with more than usual efficiency.

All human experience is remembered in that incredible instrument which we all take so much for granted — the human brain. Every frame of every film you have ever seen, every line of every book you have ever read, every distant face ever glimpsed in a crowd — all these have been miraculously filed away.

Romark proved this theory positively in a dramatic experiment carried out with the help of the *News of the World* newspaper in London and with the police authorities. Here is his account of what happened:

Crime reporter Peter Earle and photographer David Hooley attended a private screening of a film on road safety in London. The film showed an accident and its aftermath. The accident sequence lasted for less than three minutes and the action was swift.

An hour after the film ended, twenty-six questions about details shown in the film were put to Earle and Hooley. Twenty-four hours later the same questions were put to them again. Both men gave identical answers on both occasions. Earle answered fifteen questions correctly; Hooley was right in fourteen cases.

I was totally unaware of the contents of the film. Two days after the screening I was asked to hypnotize the two men who had been brought to my rooms in Newcastle specially for this purpose. I told them that, while they were under hypnosis, they would visualize the film in slow motion.

The memory of each of the newspaper men was incredibly improved under hypnosis. Three key questions, which neither could recall earlier, were now recalled in precise detail.

In the film. after the accident occurred, a witness went to a public telephone box and called the police. Earle and Hooley had been asked whether they could remember the number of the public telephone. Previously they had not been able to. Now, under hypnosis, they could.

They could also remember the number plate of a car which had been shown on the film as driving past without stopping. And they remembered the name of a dog which had run across the road and which had been called by its owner. The name? Bimbo.

This experiment was recalled by a newspaper in South Africa when I was appearing at the Lyric Theatre in Durban. As a result, my help was called for by Colonel Visser, the city's CID chief. He told me that a girl of seventeen had been brutally raped on the outskirts of Durban. This young girl had been so psychologically shocked by the attack that all conscious memory of the incident had been expunged from her mind.

At Colonel Visser's request, I hypnotized the girl and regressed her to the night in question. She was able to recall every detail. She gave specific descriptions of the three men who had been involved in the assault and told the police the make and colour of their car. The police, armed with this information, were able to make two arrests within twenty-four hours. Both men were subsequently convicted.

Perhaps the most dramatic example of the use of hypnosis in a criminal case involved the infamous Boston Strangler.

The case of the Boston Strangler is one of the most bizarre in the annals of criminology. De Salvio, the man who was eventually found guilty of the crimes which had terrorized an entire city, actually confessed to eleven murders, plus another two which the authorities didn't know about. He also admitted approximately 2,000 rapes.

He was not believed.

Eventually a hypnotist was called in. He placed De Salvio under hypnosis and regressed him to the time when he committed the eleventh murder (the facts of which had not been reported in the press). Precise details of the killing were obtained under hypnosis. Following this, De Salvio was indicted and convicted.

The *Independent Press Telegram* of Boston commented: 'Hypnosis, long used to relieve individuals of their tensions, has helped relieve an entire city of a massive fear, of hysteria bordering on panic.'

That is why it is so important that, when you programme yourself for a particular task, you do so with mental pictures of the utmost clarity and reality. The better the quality of input, the higher the standard of retention by your brain — your computer.

There is a great deal of intuitive wisdom in folkloric expressions, even though they are usually misapplied. The phrase 'The thought is father to the deed' acquires a new connotation when regarded in the context of Hypnothink.

It is a fascinating truth that children's games often lead to adult occupations. Conrad Hilton once said in an interview that when he was a child he used to play a game in which he had a lot of hotels. In adulthood he became the world's leading hotelier. In his imagination as a child he had done it all before.

Children play with soldiers and go on to seek a military career. Little girls play nurses and echo their childish instincts by joining the nursing profession later in life.

Play-acting, or visualizing, is a natural instinct in man but, like so many other vital impulses, it tends to fall into disuse in adult life.

Will-power plays no role in Hypnothink. If anything, it would have a disruptive effect. In the same way, it does no good at all just to 'think positively'. In other words, for a boxer to say to himself before a contest, 'I'm going to win' over and over again does nothing useful. It is living in a fool's paradise. But, should he approach the situation on an organized basis, by feeding specific visualized data into his brain, the possibility of winning the fight becomes a logical reality.

It is possible to apply the principles of Hypnothink to specialized areas of human endeavour — sporting activities, losing weight, stopping smoking, making public speeches, and so on. But it is also possible to change your entire personality — by seeing yourself in a new role.

To achieve this personality change, evaluate yourself as you are at present — and do it honestly. Then picture yourself as you would like yourself to be. Don't picture yourself as arrogant, powerful and egotistical because, if you do, you are not creating a real person. You must create not just the kind of person you would like to be, but the sort of person you would like to know. Don't forget that you, above all people, will have to live with the new You.

For the same reasons, when you create your improved personality, don't go to the other extreme and deliberately plan flaws in your character just to make yourself 'human'. There is no need for flaws. They are negative. You must create a positive personality.

Bear in mind that the process of Hypnothink *will not* conjure into existence an entirely new person. What it *will* do is to enable you to perfect your existing personality, shedding the weaknesses and the handicaps and fortifying and extending the qualities of strength. It will help you to become the person Nature intended you to be.

After all, why should we have been given the largest brain in creation if the intention was that we should remain inferior beings and sub-standard products?

Those of you who have read Romark's book *The Sins of the Fathers*, will be familiar with the theory that parental influence — well-intentioned though it usually is — can be severely damaging to children. It can warp, distort and stunt the personality potential. Every day therapists have continuing proof of this fact. People whose confidence has been dramatically sapped, whose inner security has been destroyed, men and women beset by a multitude of fears, anxieties and phobias, sad people whose zest for life has been stolen from them and replaced by bitter disillusionment and despair — in their thousands they are crying out for help.

But it is no longer primarily the influences of misguided parents which wreak this havoc among humanity. Now the external influences take their toll as well. As society has 'progressed', so has it become more vulnerable to the destructive effects of its own creations, such as the mass media and intensive advertising.

It is a symptom of the confusion prevalent in society that the sexual roles have become blurred — and in some cases reversed. Men see themselves in a female role; women try to become more masculine. Many people regard marriage as outmoded and unnecessary. More and more people indulge in multiple sex, group sex and mixed sexual groups as variants on the now more orthodox homosexual and lesbian relationships.

But there is no reason at all why men and women should not retain their sexual identities, happily and in a spirit of fulfilment. It is entirely possible for men and women to marry and enjoy a thoroughly rewarding life in the matrimonial state, if this is their desire, producing children and bringing them up in an atmosphere of harmony and enjoyment. Too many people feel threatened or guilty for wanting just this sort of traditional relationship. But this is all a question of Inner Face.

Your Inner Face is the touchstone of your life in every respect. If you programme yourself to have a truly happy marriage, then it will come about.

The people with a poor Inner Face are wont to say: 'I have nothing to do. I am bored.' These unfortunate people are not motivated towards a target. They have started a failure mechanism within themselves — and this kind of mechanism is self-perpetuating. It provides a justification for procrastination and avoiding work. 'Why bother?' they ask themselves. 'Why try?' They have trapped themselves on a treadmill of humdrum existence. If, by some fluke, this type of person should achieve a genuine success in some field, he cannot live with it. His instinctive reaction is one of guilt — as though he has stolen something to which he is not entitled. And this syndrome is much more widespread than most people realize.

It is essential, therefore, that you accept that you are entitled to take the credit for your own capabilities. Never feel guilty about succeeding. Real success — a target attained — cannot hurt anyone. It is a creative accomplishment and as such can only be of universal benefit.

Emotional hurt leaves emotional scars in the same way, and just as genuinely, as physical injury leaves the legacy of a physical scar. In order to programme yourself for the future you will have to seek out and recognize these scars.

When people are hurt emotionally they withdraw into themselves. But what they should do is remove those scars — rather like having cosmetic surgery — so that the Inner Face is restored to an acceptable state. The verbal imagery used by such people is indicative of their feelings. They say 'I have gone into my shell,' or 'I have built a wall around me.' A woman who has been spurned or betrayed will say: 'I'll never put myself into a position where I could be hurt by another man.'

A shell keeps things out — but it also keeps you in.

If you build a wall to keep out one hurtful thing, it will also keep away many other things — a lot of them useful and rewarding.

People with this attitude to life will not trust anyone, even if they feel an inner need to be dependent on others. They are so afraid of being rejected that they are likely to attack first, causing hurt and confusion in the object of their attack. In this way they drive away the very people to whom they find themselves attracted. It often happens, too, that those people will repel and antagonize those who would be able to give them medical or phychological help.

The irony in this sort of situation is that their fear creates the very situation which they feared in the first place — alienation.

Emotionally scarred people have an Inner Face of being unwanted and disliked. They see the world as a horrid place. Other people are there for combat, not for co-operation. They have created for themselves a world of frustration and loneliness.

Sensitivity to criticism is a sure indication of a poor Inner Face. How often have you heard people say to someone: 'Be careful what you say in front of *him.*' They have learned from experience that *he* is very quick to take offence, to see an insult where none is intended. Such a person is hurt by imagined threats to his ego. An intense exaggeration of this process will result in paranoia — a fixed delusion of danger from real or imagined threats to the ego.

This sort of attitude creates an insecurity which need not exist at all. It is necessary for us all to have some sort of ego protection — a resilience of spirit which enables us to withstand the blows which life sometimes aims at our self-esteem. But when people over-react and develop a thick layer of scar tissue to protect themselves against any future injury, they are also robbing themselves of the pleasure of sensitive feelings, of the refinements of enjoyment which are among the richest blessings of life.

When a physical injury is received, it can leave visible scar tissue because of the tension of the skin healing under pressure. If there is no tension of the skin, there will be no scar.

This applies equally to the emotions — to the mind.

In a state of emotional relaxation it is impossible to feel tension, or anger, or fear. It is medically out of the question for a relaxed person to have asthma or to suffer from a migraine headache.

Physical states of tension (or non-relaxation) come about through a person responding negatively to a particular situation which has become a source of anxiety. We have already discussed one method of inducing physical relaxation — that of visualizing the limbs as being as heavy as lead, beginning with the feet and working upwards. Another way is to sit in a chair — preferably one which has a high enough back to support your head — and have a pleasant day-dream. (For more detailed explanation of how to achieve mental relaxation, turn to Chapter 8, which deals with mental tranquillity.)

In the process of programming yourself for the future, it is necessary for you to cut out those old scars which clog up your emotions and obstruct the way for valuable sensations. How do you perform this magic surgery? For one thing, don't *forgive* people for hurtful actions against you in the past. Just *forget* them. If you forgive, rather than forget, you create a sensation of moral righteousness. This could make an even bigger scar — because it can become an aid to memory — which can become a cancer which feeds on being recalled. You recall your righteousness in having forgiven the offender — so at the same time you remember the offence and it rankles.

Never fall into the trap of forgiving someone and therefore thinking of them as being somehow indebted to you. If you do, you will find that when that debt is cancelled, you are in reality creating a new debt.

Consider an analogy. A money-lender lends someone £10 and charges £1 in interest, due on repayment in two weeks time. After two weeks the borrower has not repaid the debt. He tendered a cheque but it bounced. So the money-lender draws up a new agreement for a loan — the principal amount of £10 plus the £1 in interest which is owed, plus £1.50, which is the new interest due. The debt has now grown to £12.50. If the borrower still fails to pay, the amount will become greater at a progressively swifter rate.

What we want is not a quality which can be used as a weapon. It actually does you the world of good emotionally if the grudge is cut out completely, like a surgically removed cancer, so that the wound can heal cleanly without leaving any scars.

Unfortunately, human nature is such that it gives us pleasure to be able to feel superior by means of a sense of justified condemnation of others. It provides an opportunity for mental one-upmanship.

We must completely cancel the debt. It is not a valid debt.

We are not going to do this to be generous, or to do a favour, or to feel morally superior. We must try to understand that there is truly nothing to forgive. It was our mistake to have these negative feelings in the first place. Do not make other people responsible to you for their behaviour, so that they fall from *your* grace by not matching *your* moods and wishes.

In the same way that you forgive and forget the transgressions of others against you, you will learn to forgive yourself. Think about the nature of self-guilt. It is a wish to change history and change our actions in the past. This is manifestly impossible. Simply tear up the bounced cheque — it can't be cashed anyway. At the same time, recognize your past errors so that your brain can automatically steer clear of them as it aims for targets.

The terminology you use in your own private assessment of things can be significant. 'I have failed,' for instance. This means that you have recognized an error, a shortcoming in yourself. This knowledge can prove to be most beneficial in the future. By contrast, 'I am a failure' means that in your own mind you believe that that same error has changed you as a person.

To clarify this line of thought: if someone gets a pain in his leg we say: 'He has a pain in his leg.' We don't say: 'He is a cripple.'

We all make mistakes. It is an unavoidable aspect of human nature that we should do so. But mistakes do not have to make you a failure as a person. Be prepared to be vulnerable to error. Who isn't? Don't over-protect yourself. If you do get hurt, you can overcome it.

The essential awareness for you to retain is that you must keep your sensitivity alive in order to create.

In the world of nature, the hedgehog and the oyster are good examples of creatures which have been made virtually invulnerable in terms of their environment.

Who ever heard of a creative hedgehog? Who wants to be an oyster? Who would want to meet a skunk?

In developing your personality, in bringing it to the fore so that the rest of the world can see it — and in doing this successfully — you cannot retain any kind of false front.

What better example of a lovable personality can we find than a baby? Any baby. A baby has a personality which is instantly lovable because it has not yet learned emotional deviousness or dishonesty. It has not yet discovered guilt. It has no inhibitions.

An effective personality is an uninhibited one. The very word 'inhibit' means to restrain, to hold back. And if you hold yourself back, you are inhibiting your personality. If you are not being yourself according to your Inner Face, then it is impossible for you to express yourself.

Your sense of self-criticism should be just sufficient to guide you on to your target. It should not be potent enough to deflect you in the opposite direction. All self-criticism should be made in the spirit of 'What I am doing is wrong' — not 'It is wrong to do anything'. Self-cricitism should be subconscious and automatic. Excessive self-criticism can exacerbate a phobic condition, as in the case of stammering and bed-wetting.

As Romark explains in his books, *The Sins of the Fathers* and *The Curse of the Children,* stammerers and bed-wetters become so self-critical that they set up tensions within themselves which compel them to stammer and wet their beds.

They overcome their handicaps by *trying* to do the very things they most fear doing. A stammerer always goes over his intended speech in advance of saying it. He is usually afraid of stammering on a particular word. Invariably *that* is the word he stammers on. If he relaxes and doesn't *care* whether he stammers or not, he doesn't stammer.

Exactly the same principle applies to bed-wetting. If a bed-wetter removes self-criticism from his mind and goes to bed with a determination to wet his bed, he will find that he cannot do so.

A similar principle applies to the many people who have a worrisome hand tremor. Visualize four separate tasks — walking along a log, threading a needle, pouring a drink and putting a key in a lock. In each case the critical failure only occurs at the exact moment of doing it. You make yourself too conscious of it — and excessive tensions disrupt the performance of the act.

If the log were not floating in a river, but lying on the floor in your living room, you would have no difficulty in negotiating it. In other words, it is easy to be steady when you know you do not have to try too hard. Excessive care in doing something tends to result in doing it wrongly, or not doing it at all. You must learn to trust your spontaneity. Let the computer in your brain do the work.

When someone says 'I am self-conscious' what does he really

mean? What he is really saying is: 'I am conscious of others.' Let your communication with others be spontaneous, not inhibited, and your personality will bloom.

If you are introduced to a group of strangers and consciously think that you must try to 'make a good impression', you will automatically begin to monitor your behaviour. The immediate result is that you inhibit your creativity, which should flow uninterruptedly. You should never allow yourself to wonder what the other person is thinking of you. On the contrary — be yourself. Extend your personality to him so that he can find out what you are like. Otherwise he will never know.

The judicious use of Hypnothink will enable you to overcome all the stress situations which we have touched on here.

Picture a situation which is normally troublesome to you. Then indulge in a leisurely day-dream involving that situation. Try to imagine every possible variation of that situation — and in each case bring yourself through it with flying colours.

By this method you will remove the worrying possibility of finding yourself in a situation where you cannot cope. Once you have acquired the inner conviction that, no matter what happens in a given situation, nothing can hurt you, you will have acquired an important attribute. It is known as poise.

Romark gives you a specific example of how Hypnothink worked for one of his patients:

I was consulted by a man who had been a member of the working class of Britain all his life. Then one day he won the football pools. Suddenly he was rich beyond his comprehension.

Because he had all this money, he felt compelled to live up to it. He frequented expensive restaurants and hotels. He found himself mixing in circles which were utterly alien to him. The result was predictable. He became acutely ill at ease and suffered intense anxiety attacks.

I asked him where he used to eat before he won the pools. 'We used to go to the fish and chip shop mostly,' he said.

I counselled him to 'day-dream' himself going into his local fish and chip shop before he paid his next visit to an expensive restaurant. He did it — and it worked. He became at ease and in command.

After all — he could conceive of nothing happening in his local fish and chip shop to threaten his equanimity.

7.

Move Forward to Success

The clocks and meters of the human mind are more complex and more sensitive than we suspect. Gauges of the utmost refinement record every change for better or for worse — but all too often we do not know how to read these omens.

These warning signals of nature are much more easy to perceive and interpret in the physical sphere. A fever is a sure sign that we are running a temperature and the body has been invaded by a hostile organism. Pain is a strong and direct warning of something being amiss.

When it comes to disturbances of our emotional metabolism, the brain has its own set of warning lights which herald trouble. These include feelings of insecurity, worry of an undefined nature, moments of despair, frustration and hopelessness, fits of bad temper, often out of proportion to the apparent immediate cause. Many of these signals are cries for help and attention — an adult modification of a childish habit pattern.

A baby, for intance, will rage and scream in a tantrum — until mother comes along. The fit of temper has focused attention on the baby and brought solace in the form of mother's ministrations. The child's brain remembers this emotional triumph — a moment of success — and tries to repeat it later in life. But of course truly adult people have long since shed these basic emotional manoeuvres.

More subtle manifestations, such as an ill-defined general malaise, are, in a way, signals to us from our brain that we are off course. Perhaps we have set ourselves goals which we know to be beyond our reach. Possibly we are trying to impose a new life-style upon ourselves without the proper kind of preparation. As a result we generate within ourselves the symptoms of trouble and stress. We have no outlet for this pent-up friction, so our personality mechanism begins to malfunction.

It is astonishing how widespread — and how international — feelings of inadequacy and maladjustment are.

In California several hundred students were interviewed by an eminent psychologist. About 95 per cent of those interviewed confessed that they believed themselves to be 'different' in some way. When asked to elaborate upon this, all they could say was that they felt 'defective' — 'There is something wrong with me.'

Those who think that way react to life that way. They experience shame, fear and anxiety. These strong emotions block their capacity to live life to the full. The conscious mind is knotted with scar tissue.

It is the vogue in modern psychology to encourage the gloomy view of life shared by so many of those students. If it is possible to imbue psychiatry with an overall view of life, at present it must be thoroughly pessimistic. Instincts of self-destruction are seen and pointed out at every turn and it is considered the norm to suffer from deeply entrenched feelings of guilt and neurosis.

But so much of this unhappiness and misfortune comes from misuse of the brain.

Any machine must have a task, a function. And if it is a good machine it will do its task perfectly, but even a brand new car must be 'run in' to function properly and an unused motor will seize up with lack of use.

The human brain can be regarded as a machine for the purpose of this analogy. And it is the most potent and complex machine ever created. Feed wrong data into the human brain and you will breed and perpetuate error. Correct, positive data, on the other hand, provides the right answers to emotional problems and generates harmony.

In the persistent pursuit of improvement, we must continue to move forward. Inactivity or resigned acceptance is not the equivalent of staying in the same place. It is actually a step backwards because, while you stand still, the world and life continue on their way.

While you visualize your goal and direct your efforts towards it, think of the dilemma of the tight-rope walker. If he stays in one position he will sway and fall. He must keep going to retain his balance. So must you go forward — or fall by the wayside.

Many people create a goal for themselves, strive to reach it and, when they do, they relax. What they should do is set themselves a new target to aim for. As the saying has it: 'Happiness lies in the pursuit of a desire as much as in the fulfilment of it.'

Loneliness is a specific aspect of maladjustment. Many people who regard themselves as lonely owe their loneliness to themselves — because they do not have the confidence in themselves to believe that other people can like them. In very many cases the cause of this pervading unhappiness has been a parent.

In most cases it has been the father who has the problem, not the child. The father has not had the ability to communicate and so gives the appearance of being taciturn and surly. Because the father does not succeed in getting through to his son, the son assumes that *he* is at fault. To a young child, a parent is a form of god, without error or shortcoming.

The child's logic is as follows: 'If I can't talk to my father — who should be closer to me than any person on earth — then how can I talk to anyone? If *he* doesn't like me, how can anyone else like me?'

One of the bitter ironies in the condition of loneliness is that those who suffer from it will try courageously to smile in a bid to invite friendship. All too often, because of their inhibitions, they strangle that smile at birth, so that it gives the appearance of being a supercilious smirk — makes them appear to others to be 'stuck-up'. So the attempt to win approval has ended in disaster — has turned into an attitude more likely to antagonize than to attract.

Surprisingly, quite a few lonely people like to stay that way. They are afraid that the closeness of friendship will expose them to the searching knowledge of others, with the result that their imagined 'unworthiness' and 'inadequacy' will be discovered. It never occurs to a lonely person to make the initial overtures in a relationship. But, if that first bond of friendship can be forged, somehow they will often lose their shyness.

Another point to remember when you are remodelling your Inner Face to your new requirements is that you must not fear the possibility of making mistakes which, you think, will shatter your new image. This fear could create a pattern of uncertainty in decision making.

Accept the fact that no one can be a hundred per cent perfect. If you need to be persuaded of this fact, all you need to do to change your view is to think of the world of sport.

In cricket, even the greatest batsman in the world can be bowled out. A crack shot does not always hit the bullseye. Even the best of footballers has been known to miss a penalty kick.

People who have built for themselves a strong Inner Face do not mind admitting their mistakes. Thomas Edison said: 'Every wrong attempt I make is another step forward.'

People with a failure-orientated Inner Face blame 'bad luck' for their misadventures. They can always find a multitude of scapegoats. If all the energy wasted on these excuses for failure could be harnessed in a constructive way, we would be well on our way to success.

To sum up: In order to create a new Inner Face you must be active all the time. Don't rest on your laurels — whether real or imagined.

Set yourself positive targets — not the passive kind in which you praise yourself for *not* having done something.

Do not place your reliance on others in your efforts to achieve new goals. By tapping the mysterious forces which exist within your psyche and your brain, you will unleash reserves of power beyond your wildest dreams.

8.

A Tranquillizer is not a Pill

In an increasingly complex world, tensions are imposed upon us in a million subtle ways. That is why there is such a huge market in tranquillizers — pills designed to render you indifferent, to one degree or another, to the stresses and strains of the world. But we can take a mental tranquillizer rather than a physical one. There are methods of thought, devices of the brain, which can be used to neutralize the destructive onslaught of tension.

The purpose of a tranquillizing pill is to make us less aware of outside aggravations and to diminish our anxiety quotient. But one simple way of tranquillizing yourself is to *ignore* these stresses and strains. To fail to respond in any way to an outside influence.

As we progress from infancy to youth to adulthood we become conditioned to a huge variety of outside stimuli, differing enormously according to our individual upbringing. But for all of us there exist danger signals which induce in us a state of mind stemming from our early experiences. We have unwittingly been programmed by life. Now that we have discovered Hypnothink, we are able to reprogramme ourselves in a more desirable way.

Many people will say that at work they are confident and happy 'until I have to talk to the boss. Then I just dry up'. Others are affected by strangers, by enclosed spaces, by open spaces, by heights, by insects . . . the list is a very long one, limited only by the human imagination. For one reason or another these people were led to believe, earlier on in their lives, that those particular objects or situations were dangerous, menacing, anxiety-inducing.

This chapter will explain how you can short-circuit these responses and eliminate them altogether.

A good example of a conditioned response is what happens when someone rings your front doorbell. You get up and answer it.

But what happens if you are very tired and alone? You may ignore the bell and remain in your chair, relaxed.

You can do exactly the same in your mind. Relax! Let that doorbell ring. Ignore it. You don't have to take notice of a danger signal. After all, it is only a signal — not a compulsion. And the danger is not a valid one anyway.

Evaluate yourself to find out what your personal danger signals are. Then programme your Inner Face to ignore the signal. Your new Inner Face will ignore these signals from now on.

If you are a person who has been afraid of heights, for example, and every time you climbed a certain number of stairs you received a danger signal, you will find that this no longer happens. You are letting the doorbell ring — you are happily climbing the stairs.

Another method by which you can neutralize these danger signals is to *delay* your customary response.

Scarlett O'Hara in *Gone with the Wind* used to say: 'I won't think about that today. I'll think about it tomorrow.'

This is a very useful technique — as long as you never carry it to the extreme of never doing anything about anything! But it is a highly advantageous way of postponing an unsettling response.

If you are placed in a position where your mind is startled by some stimulus which you know will create a danger signal for you, follow the old advice and — count to ten before you do anything.

It is a delaying tactic.

If you delay your response you have time to clear your mind. This means that you don't have to follow the emotional, conditioned path of response to which you are accustomed.

As soon as you introduce relaxation to the brain you remove stress. And if you ignore the stress stimulus — that is the equivalent of the removal of stress. A lack of response equals relaxation.

When you are about to undertake some physical task, you flex your muscles. When you are about to undertake a mental task, you flex your brain. If you decide to ignore the physical task, however, you don't bother to flex your muscles. In exactly the same way, you should not bother to flex your brain at the first sign of a danger stimulus.

Let the doorbell ring!

Multitudes of people, when faced by the stresses of our modern life with its assaults upon our peace of mind and its erosion of our tranquillity, think how blissful it would be to 'get away from it all'. Psychologists call this the 'desert island syndrome' and it is one of the symptoms of the strain of present-day existence that so many people have it.

Well, there is a way by which you can 'get away from it all'. And the wonderful thing is that you don't have to go anywhere to do it.

There is a formula by which you can obtain mental relaxation whenever you require it. What you must do is build a quiet den — a hideaway — in your mind. Think in terms of a wheel. Visualize the centre of the wheel. The exact centre of a wheel is a point of absolute stillness. It remains totally static while the wheel is still; it remains totally static while the wheel revolves around it.

Think yourself into that centre. Imagine that tiny dot at the centre and at the precise centre of that dot is your own den. It is a magnificent place — the perfect reflection of your wishes and desires.

Open the door. Perhaps it is a huge oak door with a giant knocker. Perhaps it is a plastic trap door, made of a modern fibre, and it flicks back as you lift your finger in command. The door is precisely as you would wish it to be.

Go inside. The dimensions of your den are as great or small as you wish them to be. The ceilings may be high and regal or low and cosy.

Furnish it as you will. Perhaps you have a very good, old and comfortable chair in which you can achieve absolute physical relaxation. Your den can be furnished with priceless antiques, with the latest in modern glass and chrome furniture — it can have a colour television, a stereo, an all-purpose bed, or just a rug and a table. It is your dream dwelling exemplified.

This is an utterly private retreat. No one has ever set foot there and no one ever will. It exists purely within your own imagination. It is an avenue of escape from the outside world.

Find some time every day to enter your den and spend some time there.

This concept of a den at the absolute centre of a wheel blends the human necessities of belonging and yet being apart.

Within the constantly turning wheel you have not left life at all — merely withdrawn from it to a state of total tranquillity for as long as you wish. You can find peace without being left out of the forward momentum of life.

Frustrations and tensions will often build up within a person to such an extent that they have to blow off steam — just like a pressure cooker. Fill a pressure cooker with water, put it on a stove, adjust the stop-cock on top and eventually the cooker will build up so much pressure that it will explode. But if you remove that little stopper, the steam escapes with extraordinary force.

The human mind is very similar. If you build up a head of steam you must have an escape valve — otherwise there will be the equivalent of an explosion.

Many people blow off steam by losing their tempers, by shouting, by showing aggression. Now that you have your own private den, you can go into it and figuratively scream your head off if you so wish. It is your private domain — your own little world. So you release your build-up of tension without hurting either yourself or anyone else.

The presence of too much 'steam' is the cause of so much of the insomnia that we hear about today. Countless thousands of insomniacs spend restless nights in search of sleep but are unable to halt the ceaseless activity of their brains.

Before you go to bed, retreat into your den and let off steam in whatever manner you find most satisfying and most appropriate to your particular frustration. Then you will be able to get into bed with an attitude of relaxed contentment — and you will sleep.

This method of creating a highly personal den and withdrawing into it whenever necessary is a variation on the techniques of what is known as 'transcendental meditation'. It is an improvement, however, in that it is a more tangible concept. You can actually 'see' your den in your mind. You can go into your own domain where everything is pleasant and harmonious and at peace with the world.

Constant victims of the tensions of urban life are the motorists. The driver of a car must suffer many aggravations — in addition to those tensions with which he is already burdened — when he leaves home in the morning or drives back from work in the evening. These pressures manifest themselves in a dangerous and aggressive pattern of driving or, if the motorist is too responsible a person to allow his driving to be affected, he may vent his spleen on his colleagues, his staff or his family.

Before you even get into your car, retire into your own imaginary den for a few moments. Savour the peace and tranquillity of it. Put your mind into neutral. When you come out of your den and get into your car you will be a changed person.

The overwhelming advantage of this technique, of course, is that you can resort to it at any time of the day or night, no matter where you happen to be — whether you are stuck in a crowded lift, trapped on the underground, at home or at work, or jammed in a motionless phalanx of stalled cars. It only takes an instant and — hey presto, you are whisked away into a private lair where peace reigns supreme.

Do not confuse this procedure with Hypnothink. There need be no link between your activities in your den and actual elapsed time. You can go in there for five seconds or five minutes. It depends entirely on your own whim. With practice you will learn how to transport yourself into the den at the centre of your mind in an instant.

People tend to acquire a misleading perspective and to lose sight of the fact that it is the outside world which affects them. Rather, they think in terms of what occurs within their own personalities. But, in fact, it is usually some other person who impinges on your sense of well-being, or some external situation which brings about an abrasive circumstance.

Now you can alleviate the effect of these disruptive external influences by escaping into your den — into your own secret place.

One way of achieving self-tranquillization is to refuse to respond to outside influence. But there is another aspect to this. It is possible for you to invoke outside influences as a positive aid in programming.

For example, if you are overweight and you are programming yourself to become slim, picture yourself sitting in a restaurant, enjoying your permitted meal — and watching the many others around you who are overeating or eating the wrong things. They are making themselves gross and unhealthy, while you remain poised and slim. *You* are not doing what the rest are doing. It is positive abstinence.

Different people react in many different ways to crisis. For some, crises being out the best in them. Others just fall apart at the seams. This is true, too, of all pressure situations — such as intensive selling and public speaking.

The type of reaction evoked by strain depends on how the person concerned has been conditioned in earlier life. As happens in all life's situations, we are all in the process of being unwittingly programmed throughout our childhood and our youthful years.

In applying the principles of Hypnothink, we must adjust our Inner Face and programme our 'new face' in conditions of calm and harmony.

An old-fashioned and somewhat barbaric method of teaching children to swim was to throw them headlong into the water, presenting them with simple alternatives — swim or sink! As a result the children swam to survive. Survive they did, but they had no swimming technique as such. They acquired the most primitive and energy-wasting system of staying afloat.

In Hypnothink, a person prepares to make a speech, for example, by programming himself calmly and thoroughly, with no anticipation of a crisis disrupting the planned procedure. Having been programmed, however, if a crisis does occur, his brain-computer will adjust and shift accordingly, without undue strain. The crisis will be accommodated and overcome.

Because the speaker was in a state of control and equilibrium, he was in the best possible state of mind to deal with an unexpected departure from the norm.

This principle has particular relevance in the world of sport.

The sportsman should always Hypnothink aggressively to achieve positive results. If he is a footballer, it is of no use to think merely in terms of a draw. He must not even think simply of winning — but of *humbling* the other team.

This positive approach is implicit in the principles of Hypnothink.

Some people may find at first that, although they have programmed themselves well, they fail to perform satisfactorily in the situations they have made their target. They must not give up at this point. Persevere. Carry on with the same method of thought. The combined potency of correct programming and perseverance is infallible. But early capitulation to initial negative feed-back is simply a case of over-compensation which will have a negative effect.

Another source of danger which must be avoided at all costs is the negative activity of visualizing possible misadventures in the future.

The man who allows negative pictures to infiltrate the screen of his mind is creating a very involved situation with all sorts of complex possibilities.

For example, if you think: 'What would happen to my family if I got cancer?' you are embarking upon an intangible equation in which it is impossible to programme the situation.

Don't imagine things which *may* happen. Visualize that which definitely *will* happen, or which actually *has* happened.

It is vitally important that you are very aware of the fact that, once you conjure up a picture in your mind, even if it is a fuzzy outline, or a mere potential possibility, it becomes a reality as far as your brain is concerned.

Your computer does not care about the difference between imagination and reality. That is the essence of Hypnothink.

We humans have drawn many constructive examples from the study of the humble ant. And once again the ant has something to show us in its pattern of behaviour during a crisis.

In an ant-nest, bustle and activity never cease. But, if you stand on an ant-heap and damage its exterior, the ants do not react to this crisis with confusion or uncontrolled behaviour. At once all the ants in the vicinity rush to the damaged area and proceed to rebuild it. They do it quickly — but efficiently and methodically.

We can even learn from the behaviour of rats. In an American university rats were kept in a complex maze. Food was placed at various points in the maze. The supply was plentiful and the rats took their time over wandering around in search of the constantly changing sites of food. Then some starving rats were placed in the maze. Contrary to what one might expect, the starving rats took four times as long as the well-fed rats to find the food.

Crisis did not help them towards greater functional efficiency.

The lesson to be drawn from these observations is that, whatever your target, whether it be to deliver a speech, play sport, or simply to mix easily with people at a party, practise doing it in a calm and pressure-free atmosphere — and in fine detail.

A basic truth of Hypnothink is that your computer is the greatest ad-libber in the world.

Consider the analogy of a golfer practising his putting on his living-room carpet. He places the ball on the carpet and putts it into a tumbler. There are no pressures upon him. No money is at stake. There is no intensely inquisitive crowd pressing forward behind him. There are no prizes to be won.

This is the ideal setting for him to practise — to programme himself as closely as possible to perfection. Then, when he faces the reality of competitive pressure, he has the strength of calm preparation behind him, and his computer will be able to adjust accordingly.

A cardinal rule of Hypnothink is that you must always rehearse under non-pressure conditions. Don't prepare for crises. Don't even consider the possibility of it.

If you tell your brain clearly and concisely and precisely what it is that you want to happen, your brain will ad-lib and create a way for it to happen whatever the circumstances that prevail at the time.

9.

Tune in to a Good Programme

One Sunday afternoon Eddie Williams and his friend went for a drive out in the country. During the afternoon their car had a puncture in the back wheel, so they got out to change the wheel. Eddie's friend took out the spare wheel and was trying to put it in place when the car slipped off the jack. It came down on top of his hands, trapping them against the tyre.

Eddie, standing behind him, leaned across, grabbed the chassis and lifted the two-and-a-half ton weight of the car off his friend's hands.

Now Eddie would be the first to admit that he is not a particularly muscular man and he has never been enthusiastic about exercise or physical fitness. What he said, soon after the event, was: 'When I thought afterwards about what I had done, I could not believe that it had been possible. But I *had* done it. The need to remove that tremendous destructive weight from my friend's fingers was so urgent that I unleashed total concentration and performed the necessary task without questioning for even a split second whether I could do it or not.'

Human experience is full of such examples of 'impossible' feats of strength. A woman, for instance, will perform an apparently superhuman act in order to rescue her child from danger.

The hidden and often unsuspected reserves of power in our brain and body are tapped in a surpassing moment of emotional intensity. But what we must realize is that we can harness this source of power on a calculated and conscious level.

There was a fairly recent example, drawn from life, of Hypnothink in action in the sphere of physical prowess.

British television told the story of an innkeeper in Southampton who drank innumerable pints of beer every day and lived on pork pies. His doctor, who frequented the pub, accused him of being totally unfit and of abusing his body.

The doctor was a keep-fit fanatic. He ate a balanced diet, didn't drink, didn't smoke and kept in training. Thirty years previously the publican had been a professional cyclist. Now, annoyed by the doctor's charge that he had lost his fitness, he challenged the medical man to a race.

Interviewed on television, the publican said that the doctor didn't stand a chance of winning. Having once been a first-class cyclist, he said, he knew his job and was sure that he could win again. And the only training he was going to do was drink more beer.

The doctor, on the other hand, made a point of emphasizing that the issue was one of physical fitness alone. He ran around a playing field every night and kept up his balanced diet and practised on his cycle.

The race took place. The publican won easily, even stopping halfway to sink a pint of beer. Romark recalls:

When I saw that innkeeper on television prior to the race, I was convinced that he would win the race because his attitude was perfect Hypnothink. He was buoyed up by the knowledge of past success and he had Hypnothought himself into winning, in spite of all the obvious indications against him.

In the process of acquiring a correct programming, there are various attitudes which can mar the procedure.

The question of conventional morality is one which confuses some people. When programming oneself, they say, to be a 'good' person, how does one specify what is right and what is wrong?

What are morals? And, in any case, who are we to judge? Without delving too deeply into the complex subject of ethical morality, what we need to remember for the purposes of programming is that 'right' and 'wrong' can be relative to the particular situation.

For example, we are taught that it is morally wrong to strike someone. But it is not morally wrong — in fact it is an action applauded by society — if, for instance, you strike someone who is in the process of attacking an old lady.

Don't be too hidebound in your approach to the matter of morality, therefore. Your own conscience is as accurate a guide as any in these matters.

Another aspect of morality which occurs among some of our

patients who apply Hypnothink for the first time is the question of whether or not they 'deserve' the rewards which the system brings them.

These unfortunate people are crippled by an excessively puritanical upbringing. To create success for themselves the Hypnothink way, by programming and adjustment of their Inner Face, seems to them to be too easy. They feel that there is not enough effort involved and, as a result, they cannot 'deserve' the rewards which flow from the procedure. This attitude of course is based on entirely wrong conceptions. There can be nothing dishonourable or evil about adjusting your personality for the better. Happiness cannot be culpable.

Yet another facet of repressive upbringing is a general timidity which handicaps people in many different walks of life.

A common syndrome among show-business folk is stage fright. Before going on stage to entertain their audience, many actors and variety artists are caught in the grip of savage anxiety. In some extreme cases it ends by rendering the artist incapable of performing.

Stage fright is a fear of being punished for 'showing off'. Most children, at some time or another, are told to be quiet. In extreme instances they are told that they should only speak when they are spoken to. It is considered to be the norm of average society that it is not done to try to be the centre of attention. In normal social intercourse one is respectful of other people's contribution to the conversation and waits for the right moment to interject or respond. In show business, however, another code of behaviour comes into play.

One of the most popular comedians in the history of British entertainment was Max Miller, who was known as the Cheeky Chappie because he would deliberately say provocative things to his audience. One of the most highly paid comedians in the United States is Don Rickles who has made a fortune out of insulting his audience.

But, leaving aside the realm of entertainment, a host of people leading ordinary lives away from the limelight have what one could describe as stage fright about living. They have a preconditioned timidity — a fear that, if they stick their neck out, someone will chop off their head.

To these people we would say, adopt as your motto: 'Speak before you think.' This reverses the conventional advice, but in your case it would be advantageous.

Some people stammer over their speech. Other people stammer in a symbolic way about the act of living.

The person who stammers over words does so because of the worry about the *possibility* of stammering. If he were simply to rush into speech he would never stammer.

Those who stammer emotionally — who are hesitant about revealing their emotions and thoughts — will find it is much more effective if they can express themselves directly.

If you pause for too long, contemplate too deeply, weigh up all the pros and cons, you inhibit the expression of your personality. This act of inhibition, in itself, creates an adjustment to your Inner Face. What you should do is simply act, by yourself, and leave it to your brain — your computer — to make the automatic corrections which will keep you on course.

How often do people look back on some tense moment or some confrontation with another and say: 'If only I had thought of it at the time, I would have said . . .' If you are programmed correctly, you will say the right things — and at the right time.

The human personality is an inestimably complicated mechanism. The problems presented by life are innumerable But to every problem there is a solution — and Hypnothink encompasses them all.

In the course of our clinical work, we meet patients from all walks of life. Some are very rich, others are poor. Many are from somewhere in between. Some are professional people; others work with their hands, or as clerks, or are members of the service industries. They represent a complete cross-section of society.

Great wealth does not protect you from being assailed by feelings of inadequacy. Being poor does not make you immune from anxiety. And rich and poor, young and old alike, can be stricken by a grinding lack of self-confidence. A large proportion of our patients have problems which are confidence-orientated.

A wonderfully encouraging and uplifting truth about applying the principles of Hypnothink is the fact that it produces evident results right from the beginning. Hypnothink 'clicks' with people at once. They have an instinctive recognition of its truths. There is an emotional trigger response.

A typical patient will come in and say: 'I've come to see you because life is just not worth living. You are my last resort.' The pressures which have brought them to this low ebb vary encormously, but the root causes are almost invariably to be found in the influences exerted on them by their parents.

There have even been people in their mid-forties who have been brought to see us by their parents, just as though they were still children. And in an important emotional sense they *are* still children, because their parents have kept them that way.

Many patients suffer from lack of confidence, an inability to adjust to society, a general anxiety state. They are, to use their own terms, 'too highly strung' and 'excessively nervous'. As we always explain to them, the emotion of nervousness can be a source of additional strength.

Before a crisis — and during it — it is normal to experience a sense of nervousness. This emotion releases extra reserves of energy within us in order that we can cope with the crisis. Nervousness is usually thought of as meaning fear, but it can also mean anger and it can also be synonymous with an occasion of courage. Therefore it is misguided to think of nervousness as a weakness. Regard it as an extra reserve of strength to be used by your brain computer as it sees fit.

Before Judy Garland went on stage she used to work herself up into a state of semi-frenzy, a mood of high intensity — in other words, a condition of intense nervousness, but *controlled* nervousness.

Liza Minelli, Judy Garland's daughter, employs the same calculated technique to induce a mood of semi-ecstasy before she goes on stage. Because of this, she becomes an emotional cauldron on stage and her power and passion spill over to enrich the enjoyment of her audience.

To get a more positive perspective of nervousness, think of the terms used by commentators when talking of race horses. They refer to them being 'on their toes' or 'high-spirited'.

Nervousness is 'high spirits'. You are imbued with an excess of nervous energy just waiting to be used. What you have to learn to do is to channel that energy to your advantage.

The positive value of that sort of nervousness in the entertainment world is well known.

On the first night of a new show a theatre has an atmosphere which is loaded with an emotional charge — a form of human electricity. But after the show has been running for some time the level of excitement tends to drop. Nervousness has evaporated —

and with it has gone that intensity of emotion. Dullness has taken its place.

The important thing, however, is to evaluate the crises which crop up in your life because an *excess* of nervousness can be the cause of tension and anxiety. This nervous energy has nowhere to go, so it builds up the pressure within you.

One way of ensuring that you do not manufacture an excess of nervous energy to cope with a critical situation is to think of the problem as reaching its worst conclusion. This will have the effect of making the problem less bad — because the very worst never seems to happen. Because of your excessively gloomy anticipation, the fact that things are not as bad as you expected them to be should be a cause for happiness.

(Don't, however, confuse this process of evaluation with the technique of programming. What we are suggesting here is no more than a device of oblique thinking which might prove useful to some. Those of you who have any doubts about it should refrain from its use.)

We all have a natural tendency to exaggerate our crises. How common a phrase is 'to be scared to death'. But, if we allow ourselves to be disproportionately afraid of what are, in effect, minor crises, too many of us may fall victim to the common ailments of modern living and suffer from ulcers or even heart attacks. This is yet another sign of the times.

A good rule of thumb whenever you enter a crisis period is, once again, to reverse the usual cliché and tell yourself: 'I have everything to gain and nothing to lose'.

After you have put yourself through the process of self-programming, is there any way to establish the degree of success you have achieved?

Unfortunately there is no foolproof test. It would be nice if we could look through a peephole and scrutinize our Inner Face to see if it has been programmed correctly.

A reasonably reliable guide, however, is the state of your emotions immediately afterwards. If you feel 'good' — successful, confident, mildly elated — then you are geared for success. If you are geared for failure, you will feel that too.

Once you can feel, or emotionalize, that sensation of success, you can do no wrong. It is a sensation well known to sportsmen.

They call it the 'winning feeling'. And so it is.

In order to conjure up the taste of success, it is quite effective to call on the memory of minor triumphs. Think back to successes of any kind — no matter how small they might seem to you at first. Dwell on that sensation. Try to remember the texture of the emotion. Almost taste it in your mouth. Remember that time when you were inspired to say exactly the right thing to the right person at just the right moment.

The successes you recall do not have to have any relevance at all to the target for which you are programming yourself. All you seek is the general sensation of success.

That feeling of success, in fact, is one which should be impressed upon the minds of our children from their earliest days. If a youngster is given a reasonably easy task to do — one which requires some effort, but is clearly within his capabilities — he will immediately experience the success emotion of completing the task with relative ease.

Already he will have the basis of the confidence upon which he can build an entire lifetime's attitude. He will be a winner instead of a loser if this initial success is sustained and nurtured with care and sensitivity by his parents.

Think of the old sayings you know: 'I could feel it in my bones' and 'it was printed on my mind'. Hypnothink has been around — but in an unconscious, uncontrolled and undirected way — for centuries.

Now — at last — we are consciously at the controls.

For those who seek rational justification of these claims, there have been a wide range of controlled experiments in various parts of the world which appear to prove conclusively that negative emotions and positive thoughts have a strong — and measurable — effect on the human body.

Tests of emotional telepathy have been carried out by the team of Dr Lutsia Pavlova, electro-physiologist at the University of Leningrad, mathematician Dr Genady Sergeyev of the A. A. Utomski Laboratory, which is run by the Soviet military authorities, and biologist Dr Edward Naumov.

These pioneering researchers found that electro-encephalograph waves changed dramatically when a telepathic recipient was given successive emotions of a negative character. In fact, the Soviet telepath, Nikolaiev, has said: 'There is one kind of test I really hate

— the test with negative emotions. That can sometimes make me sick for hours.'

These Russian scientists have proved that negative emotions have a disastrous effect on human physiology as well as psychology. The mind responds in a marked way — but so does the body.

Equally, cheerful positive thinking helps the body to strengthen and improve its resources.

Research carried out in 1956 by Drs S. Serov and A. Troskin of Sverdlovsk demonstrated that the number of white blood cells rose by 1,500 after they had suggested positive emotions to the patients. After the impressing of negative emotions, the white cells decreased by 1,600. White blood cells, or leucocytes, are one of the body's main defences against disease.

Dr Pavlova reported: 'Transmission of several successive emotions of a negative character called up the appearance of cross-excitation of the brain. It changed the spontaneous ECG character to the tired state of the brain dominated by slow, hypersynchronized waves of the delta and theta type.'

Dr Pavlova notes that 'receivers themselves experienced unpleasant bodily sensations and strong head pains'.

After telepathic transmission of positive emotions, such as calmness and cheerfulness, the ECG became normal once again within one to three minutes — the unpleasant bodily symptoms also disappeared. (*Psychic Discoveries Behind the Iron Curtain*).

10.

Hypnotism is a Game

Hypnotism has always held a special fascination for the public, ever since the German physician, Friedrich Anton Mesmer, wrote in 1775 about the success of his experiments in inducing an extraordinary state of the nervous system. Mesmer claimed that he could control the actions and thoughts of the people subjected to his influence.

The more commonly used term 'hypnotism' was coined in 1834 from the Greek word 'hypnos' — meaning 'sleep'.

Popular literature and films have created a public conception of hypnotism which is a combination of lurid sensationalism and macabre inaccuracy.

Mesmer's statement that a 'mesmeree' — or someone in a state of mesmerism — became the complete chattel of the controller was frightening enough. But hypnotism became linked in the public mind with the occult, the supernatural, extra-sensory perception and that whole area of psychic activity which has attracted so much international attention in the last decade.

In the Soviet Union hypnotism has few of the connotations which exist in the West. The Russians have been exploring the possibilities of hypnotism since the turn of the century. It is in common use in medical and psychological practice. Its use as a tool of science is widespread.

For example, Dr V. N. Finne, a hypnotist working with Dr Leonid L. Vasiliev, conducted an experiment with telepathic influences upon a hypnotized woman, Kouzmina, who had suffered hysterical paralysis of her left side for years. She was given exceedingly strong spoken suggestions while under hypnosis — and she moved her paralysed arm and leg.

Dr Vladimir L. Raikov, a Moscow hypnotist, has conducted some audacious experiments with artificially induced 'reincarnation' in order to stimulate latent talent.

In one such case he hypnotized a young woman physics student at Moscow University. The girl had no interest in art, but Raikov persuaded her under hypnosis that she was the reincarnation of a renowned Russian painter.

After twenty-five hypnotic sessions over a three-month period, that girl became an accomplished artist — not a genius, but certainly equivalent to a professional illustrator.

Raikov does not use the conventional deep hypnotic trance for experiments of this kind. He encourages what he describes as 'active trance'.

The well-known Soviet psychologist, Dr K. K. Platonov, commented on this type of experiment. 'Developing drawing ability is only a partial example of more general laws. There is much talk about studying the latent powers of man's psyche, which science has demonstrated are unusually great.'

Chinese medicine, which has a tradition of many centuries, holds the concept of man, his body, his mind and his environment as constituting a whole. This view has it that man's body has two kinds of energy — electrical and what they choose to call Vital Energy.

Although quite distinct from electrical energy, Vital Energy is similar in behaviour and is polarized in negative and positive aspects. A human's Vital Energy, it is believed, fluctuates according to states of mind and changes of mood. There is a close association between mental and physical states.

Of course this mind-body link is categorized in the West as psychosomatic — a mental lesion or disturbance having a discernible effect in the body. A negative state of mind, in other words, acts on the Vital Energy like a poison and will finally work its way through to the physical form as a sickness.

The Chinese believe, equally, that a physical aberration can result in a mental malformation.

Chinese acupuncture has gained acceptance by Western medicine in the past few years. It is a tenet of acupuncturism that Vital Energy links man with the cosmos. Acupuncture is based on the concept of utilizing these energy channels which exist in the human physique.

The Czechs have another word for it — 'bio-energy' or 'psychotronic energy'. Indian yoga has its own term — *Prana*. And the Russians prefer to refer to it as 'bio-plasmic energy'.

But, whatever the terms used, the world's scientists have reached an acceptance of the fact that there is much more to the human being than his simple physical form.

Surely it is possible, therefore, to tap the strength and vitality of the universe? This is a heroic view of man, as a creature integrated into a cosmic equation — someone who can tune in to the stars as well as to the person sitting next to him.

As an expert hypnotherapist, Romark has conducted many experiments over a period of years and has his own views:

What is hypnotism? I choose to think of it as a game which is played by two people — the hypnotist and his subject.

The rules of the game are laid down by the subject, so that there is no question of the subject being in the hypnotist's power. For example, if the hypnotist said, 'Take off your clothes,' and the subject didn't like the idea of doing so, he would merely wake up. It is quite true that a hypnotist cannot make a subject do anything which is against the basic instincts of his nature.

Some subjects would acquiesce to the hypnotist's suggestions out of a spirit of exhibitionism, but if ever there arose any serious conflict on a question of morality or ethics, the subject's viewpoint would always prove to be the dominant one.

In my stage act I used to persuade a volunteer from the audience that he was Frankenstein's monster and I would send him among the audience to 'strangle' people. He would act out the part with enthusiasm and would actually go up to people and put his hands around their necks. But he wouldn't squeeze because it was not in his nature to do so. (After many years of hypnotic experiment, both publicly and privately, I had become convinced that people playing this game of hypnotism never became really violent, although they may be perfectly willing to act out the pretence of violence. This pattern of behaviour proved so consistent that I decided it was safe to incorporate an episode of this type in my stage show.)

I have conducted many experiments with good hypnotic subjects. I have regressed them, while in a trance, to childhood, back to the foetal state in their mother's womb and even back to what purport to be previous lives. I have also sent people into the future.

Hypnotic experiments are generally capricious, however, and it is difficult to repeat an experiment and achieve the same results as before.

A good example of this inconsistency is an experiment I tried with a young woman who proved to be a remarkably good subject.

At a meeting in a private home I hypnotized her and then went into another room, touched one record out of a collection of thousands, and one book out of hundreds in an enormous bookcase.

I then returned to the other room and asked the girl to come with me and identify the objects I had touched. She did so unhesitatingly. This was not the sort of experiment which has any clinical validity, of course, but it demonstrated to me that there had been effective telepathy while the subject was in an hypnotic trance.

When I tried to repeat the experiment with the same subject at a later stage, however, it was a complete failure. This proved to be the pattern with other good hypnotic subjects. When hypnotized for the first time they were able to emulate the feat. But not subsequently.

Another example of telepathy occurring quite unexpectedly took place during one of my television shows for the BBC.

I had an entire football team — the Bolton Wanderers — as my guests before a studio audience.

The idea was that, by trickery, I would pretend to read their minds. But something went wrong with the props and, as a result I scored zero out of ten. Of course we had to do it again — and it was not possible to rig the props again in front of everyone present. So I went through the entire performance again — and this time, using Hypnothink, I scored ten out of ten.

Hypnothink in Action: Case Histories

11.

'The Green-Eyed Monster'

Gerry Carstairs was convinced that he was, without question, quite the luckiest man alive. He stretched out on the bed, folded his hands behind his head and watched, with a sensation of delight mingled with affection, the naked body of his wife as she walked away from him.

They had just made love for the second time that day. Lucille's long legs stepped across the carpet and her superb figure undulated in that way which always made him feel a little quivery somewhere down in the pit of his stomach. Her tawny-chestnut hair fell to the middle of her back.

Lucy, his bride of only two weeks, was going to the kitchen to make coffee.

She stopped in the doorway, turned and gave him a saucy wink.

He grinned back at her. 'Lucy' he thought, 'I love you!' And to think that a mere six months ago he had not even met her. They had been attracted to each other at once and he had virtually made up his mind within a matter of days that he wanted to marry her.

They had been inseparable from the very beginning. Now they had been on honeymoon for a fortnight and had hardly spoken to another soul in that time. And yet, he thought now with pleasure and satisfaction, not for one moment had he felt bored or restless. Lucy was the perfect companion. She was merry and talkative, but capable of relaxing into silence with him.

He glanced at his watch. They were going out tonight to see a Barbra Streisand film, a comedy, and they would have to leave in about half an hour.

Idly Gerry picked up the new copy of *Time* which he had bought at the corner bookstall earlier when he had gone there to fetch a packet of cigarettes. He paged through it. There was a colour spread of pictures showing the new bathing costumes from the Continent.

Lucy placed his coffee down next to him and eased herself under his arm. He turned the magazine to show her the pictures. 'Look at that,' he said, pointing to a bikini so small that it was hardly visible. 'You'd look fantastic in one of those.'

Lucy didn't answer, but stirred her coffee vigorously.

'We'll have to get ready,' she said, 'or we'll be late.'

'I know,' he said. He put the magazine down, ignored his coffee and reached out for his wife. She slipped away from him.

'No Gerry,' she said. 'We have to go.'

As they got out of the taxi and joined the flow of pedestrians, Gerry looked about him expectantly.

He began silently to count off the seconds. One, two, three, four, five . . . he caught the familiar reaction from an oncoming man — the sudden movement of the head, the widening eyes, the slow approving grin and then the covert expression as the man tried to be a little discreet. Not all of them bothered to be discreet, of course. Many simply ogled Gerry's wife openly in the fashion of the Italian men they had encountered on their honeymoon.

Ever since the day he had first taken Lucy out, Gerry had been conscious of her primitive effect on the male sex. Everything about her was striking — her flaming hair, her beautiful figure, the way she dressed.

Now the reaction was par for the course. Gerry grinned, enjoying the sensation his wife caused. He glanced at Lucy. As usual, she seemed utterly unaware of the attention she drew from every quarter.

As they stepped across the pavement, Lucy slipped her hand through his and Gerry stood a little taller. This is my wife, he thought proudly, and squeezed her hand.

They joined the queue for tickets and the couple in front of them glanced back at them. The man, a lad of about nineteen, gave Lucy a quick once-over. His approval was obvious. His girlfriend glared at him and then at Lucy and Gerry and then turned her back on them both. She began to talk softly to her boyfriend and he bent over to hear what she was saying.

Gerry smiled again. He was in a fine good humour. They moved up to the box office and he bought two tickets.

'Is it going to be a full house?' he asked the girl.

'Not this session, sir,' she said, smiling politely at him through the glass of the cubicle. 'The later show should be packed, though.'

'Thank you,' he said. They moved on through the foyer and found their seats in the dim warmth of the cinema.

The film began and Gerry slipped into the mood of it at once. It was a Bogdanovich film, and he liked that director's comedy touch.

Lucy snuggled up against him in the darkness and put her head on his shoulder. He bent down to her. 'Can you see all right?' he asked.

'Yes darling', she whispered — though he couldn't understand how she could possibly see anything of the screen from that position. At any rate, it didn't matter as long as Lucy was content.

As the film progressed, Gerry chuckled and occasionally let out a roar of laughter. He liked Barbra Streisand and in this role she was at her best, her abrasive Bronx humour much in evidence.

At one point, as Streisand dominated the screen, he let out a real belly laugh.

He felt Lucy's fingers disengage from his hand abruptly. He felt for her hand again in the dark. 'I'm sorry darling,' he said, trying to control his amusement. 'I didn't mean to make so much noise.'

Her clenched hand slowly relaxed in his grip. He returned his attention to the film and Lucy put her head back on his shoulder. But Gerry was careful not to laugh too uproariously after that.

When the film was over, he and Lucy went through to the lounge bar for a drink. Their seats were close to the exit door and they were lucky enough to get two of the high stools at the bar. Gerry ordered their drinks and he and Lucy began to discuss the film. While he was being effusive about the comic qualities of the cast, he noticed Lucy's eyes shift away from him as she looked over his shoulder. He turned round and saw a tall, pretty girl trying to balance a long drink in her right hand and light a cigarette at the same time.

'Here,' he said impulsively, 'let me.' And he offered her a light from his cigarette lighter. She took it thankfully.

By now scores of people had surged into the small bar and it was packed.

'Why don't you take my seat?' said Gerry. 'Then you'll be able to get yourself organized.' The girl slid gratefully on to the stool and Gerry moved closer to Lucy and put his arm around her. He was still in a mood of joyful exuberance and he ordered another two drinks.

It was time for celebration, he thought.

He turned to offer the new drink to Lucy and was astonished to see that her face was set in hard lines.

'I want to go home,' she said.

'But —' he was flabbergasted. 'But, let's finish our drinks.'

'I want to go now,' she insisted. 'Please Gerry, let's go.' Lucy's lips were trembling and she looked as though she were about to burst into tears. Gerry felt enormous concern for her.

'What's the matter darling?' he asked, putting the untouched drinks back on the counter and hurrying after her. 'Are you feeling ill? Tell me what's wrong.'

I'm perfectly all right, thank you,' said Lucy coldly, looking straight ahead of her and walking off with the determination of a tank heading for a battle.

Gerry felt idiotic. He saw heads turn to watch the spectacle of the beautiful woman marching across the room with a man following behind at an awkward stumbling run. Anger flashed through him at the senselessness of this sudden dash for home. He was totally bewildered. What on earth was the matter with Lucy? He'd never known her to behave like this before.

He could literally feel her hostility towards him.

When Lucy had left her honeymoon bed earlier that day to make a cup of coffee for her husband, she felt so choked with emotion that she didn't trust herself to speak. At the door she turned to look back at Gerry, his husky figure sprawled out on the big double bed, hands behind his head as he smiled at her.

The sight of him brought such a surge of feeling within her that she felt the sting in her eyes. She gave Gerry a wink and turned away quickly.

As she busied herself in the kitchen, Lucy thought for the umpteenth time that this must be the happiest period of her life. Ever since she had met Gerry her life had been transformed. They had been together constantly. For the last two weeks they had been virtually alone together, and totally engrossed in one another.

She thought back to their love-making a little earlier. Although the actual act of love was exciting and intensely pleasurable, she much preferred the long minutes afterwards when Gerry lay there and held her in his arms.

When he cradled her so gently she felt safe and secure and

protected from the world. Time stood still. Nothing mattered. The outside world ceased to exist for her. Her universe was encompassed by Gerry's strong encircling arms.

Lucy took the cups of coffee on a tray back into the bedroom. Gerry was smoking and looking at a magazine. Lucy placed the tray on the side table and insinuated herself under his arms.

She caught a glimpse of the magazine Gerry was reading. He was looking at photographs of girls in micro-costumes. She felt an emptiness in her stomach. Why was Gerry looking at pictures of scantily clad women? Wasn't she pleasing him sexually? She experienced a dreadful sense of anxiety and imminent loss. At once her mind explored every possible area of weakness within her — anything which might have disappointed her husband. She had been putting on a bit of weight lately, she thought. Contentment, perhaps? Oh, my God, she thought, I'm getting fat and losing my figure.

She eased herself away from Gerry and picked up her cup of coffee. He said something to her as he waved the magazine about, but she didn't register the meaning of the words. She was trying to keep her composure. She stirred her coffee vigorously, making more noise than she would normally have done.

'We'll have to get ready,' she said in a businesslike tone, 'or we'll be late.'

They were going to the cinema that night to see some film Gerry was enthusiastic about. A Barbra Streisand film.

By the time they had dressed and Gerry had kissed her a few times in his bearish, affectionate way, Lucy felt more relaxed. At least they were just going to the cinema and it wouldn't be long before they were back home together and happy again, she thought.

As they left the taxi, she hooked her arm through Gerry's and let him steer their way through the pedestrians outside the cinema. She noticed, as she always did, that several of the girls passing by gave Gerry an approving glance. Bitches! she thought angrily. They can see he's mine and they still try to give him the eye!

She was still seething as they found their place in the queue for the box office. She clung even closer to Gerry's arm as they edged slowly forward.

The girl in the box office had harsh blonde hair, badly dyed, and her blouse was so low-cut that it left very little to the imagination.

As Lucy and Gerry came to the office, the girl fluttered her eyelashes at Gerry and gave him a big, false smile. Gerry said something to her and the girl bloomed under his attention. She gave him the full candle-power of her smile — and Lucy could have sworn that she noticeably thrust out her bosom. Lucy glanced up quickly at Gerry's face and, to her horror, saw that he was smiling. He was taken in by that cow, she thought. She felt angry, but the anger was overwhelmed by another sensation — one of loss. Once again she had that awful, empty feeling in her stomach.

Gerry led the way to their seats and they sat down. Almost at once the lights dimmed and the film began. Lucy held on to Gerry's arm and put her head on his shoulder. She could only see half of the screen, but she wasn't interested in the stupid film. She would stay here like this until the film was over and they could go back home again.

Gerry kept laughing and it began to irritate her. She lifted her head a bit to see the screen better, but she couldn't work out why he found it all so funny. Then Lucy realized that he was laughing most when Barbra Streisand came on the screen.

At one point Gerry's shoulder lurched under her as he slapped his thigh and let out a great belly-laugh. 'Isn't she terrific?' he said, bending to whisper to her.

Lucy wrenched her hand out of his. So she's terrific, is she? she thought grimly. That hateful, hateful woman up there on the screen! What was wrong with Gerry, that he should get so ridiculously excited about a stupid woman like that when he had her, Lucy, here with him?

She heard Gerry muttering quietly to her: 'I'm sorry darling,' and she gradually allowed him to reclaim the warmth of her hand.

Lucy ignored the rest of the film. She kept her head firmly on Gerry's shoulder and clutched his arm. No one can get at him, she thought, while he's here with me. Her anger against Barbra Streisand sustained her in a fever of passionate love for Gerry throughout the rest of the film.

When the film was over and the lights went up, Gerry suggested that they go through the lounge and they made their way through a handy exit. A red-head nearby smiled brazenly at Gerry. They found two seats at the long bar and Gerry bought the drinks. He insisted on talking about the film and Lucy found this irritating but she pretended to listen attentively.

She finished her drink and put it down on the counter. She turned back and was amazed to see the red-head bearing down on them with a drink in her hand. Lucy glared at the woman, almost willing her to go away.

Just then Gerry turned around and stood up and — to Lucy's amazement — he began to talk to the red-head, who was at once all smiles and coy glances and arch looks.

Lucy was even more astonished when Gerry offered this woman — a total stranger — his seat. The red-head looked up at Gerry and put her hand on his shoulder as she slid on to the stool, showing a lot of unnecessary leg as she did so.

Lucy was so angry that she thought she was going to explode. She had never been so humiliated!

Gerry, her husband of only two weeks, had been doing nothing all evening but flirt outrageously with every woman in sight. Lucy began to tremble and she was afraid that she was going to cry.

Gerry obviously couldn't love her any more. She looked bitterly at her husband. He was smiling as he leaned across and spoke to the barman.

Well, it wasn't really a surprise, she thought with savage despair. She had known all along that it couldn't last and that Gerry would leave her eventually. But she hadn't really expected it to happen so soon. Two weeks!

What a lovely married life she had had — for two blissful weeks. Well, she wasn't going to stay here any longer and be humiliated and made a fool of for all the world to see.

'I want to go home,' she said, trying to keep her voice steady. She felt her face set into stern lines. Gerry started mumbling something about finishing the drinks — the drinks! My God! All he could think of at a time like this was having a drink!

'Let's go,' she said and rose from the stool and hurried towards the exit. She was afraid that she would begin to cry and attract even more attention.

The trip home was a nightmare for both of them — although for completely different reasons . . .

Gerry, the loving husband, was horrified to see his dream-come-true, his blissful marriage, transformed into a nightmare — and a nightmare which defied any logical explanation. In the taxi Lucy sat with mouth clenched in a thin line of temper and refused even to acknowledge his words of affection and endearment.

For one terrifying moment Gerry thought that his wife must be in the throes of a nervous breakdown. Her face had the pinched, drawn look of neurosis — or at least of neurosis as he imagined it to be.

Lucy, for her part, sat in a loneliness which her husband would have been appalled to experience. She felt utterly isolated. Her husband, her only source of love and warmth and safety in a world she regarded as hostile, had proved to be an enemy — a betrayer.

By the time Gerry had paid the taxi driver and they had found the privacy of their own home again, both their moods had changed in an important way.

Gerry was angry now, but he also had the glimmer of perception. Having gone back over the night, he remembered that every point at which he had perceived cold or distant behaviour from his wife had been one at which their progress had coincided with the presence of another woman.

She can't be jealous, he thought, and instantly relief ran through him. It was so absurd, it was laughable.

At just that moment Lucy turned on him. Her insecurity had been transmuted into vicious anger, bolstered by a sense of her own imagined humiliation.

She accused Gerry of being unfaithful to her, of being interested only in sex, of shaming her in public by his flagrant reaction to every woman who showed any interest in him.

'You're sick, Gerry,' she said accusingly. 'Do you know that?' Her eyes, so tender just a short while ago, were accusing now. 'Only a sick person would carry on the way you have tonight.'

Gerry looked at his beautiful, disturbed wife. For the first time he saw the agony of her insecurity. And he felt great compassion for her.

'Do you want me to go and see someone?' he asked.

'Yes,' she said firmly. 'I think it's the only way.'

'All right,' said Gerry. 'But I'll only go if you come and talk to the doctor with me.'

Hypnothink in Action

The case of Lucy and Gerry was a fine example of how every human being's Inner Image colours his or her perception of life.

People who participate in the objective reality of life perceive it through the distorting prism of their own anxieties and insecurities.

The dramatized account you have just read was drawn from a real-life case history of two young people (naturally we have not given their real names) and shows just how ordinary everyday situations, common to all young couples, evoked utterly differing responses from each of them.

How is it that two people, genuinely in love and well attuned to each other's sensibilities, should be able to lose touch with each other so completely?

The reason was simply that each of them had an Inner Face with quite a different focus.

Gerry, for example, was a normal young man, proud of his wife, not troubled by jealousy because of his confident assumption (fully justified in this case) that his wife returned his love and because of his personal knowledge that she was not by nature a coquette or a flirt.

When Gerry took his wife to the cinema, he noticed the admiring glances she drew but he did not regard this as in any way a threat to his security. In a very masculine way he was proud that such an obviously desirable woman should adorn his arm. He was a normally gregarious and sociable person and he behaved in precisely that manner throughout the evening. He showed his wife a picture of a girl in a bikini which he thought would suit her. He asked a routine question of the girl in the box office. He laughed at Barbra Streisand because he thought she was witty and amusing and he offered his seat at the bar to the red-head because he was by nature a courteous man.

Lucy's Inner Face, of course, was in profound contrast to Gerry's.

Lucy was an extremely attractive and alluring woman but quite lacking in self-confidence due to her emotional insecurity. Because of this, she read quite a different significance into the happenings of that evening at the cinema.

She sincerely believed that every other woman had designs on Gerry.

When he looked at the picture of the girl in the bikini, she construed that as a lustful interest in the models wearing the swimsuits. She really believed that he had been flirting with the box office attendant. Gnawing insecurity even spurred her on to the absurdity of experiencing bitter pangs of jealousy because her husband was responding to a film actress's posturings on the screen.

Because of her lack of self-esteem, it did not occur to Lucy that she, more than her husband, was the object of admiring glances from others. She did not expect men to admire her. In her own view she was not admirable.

To find out why Lucy had such a deplorable Inner Face, we hypnotized her and regressed her into her childhood.

The pattern we uncovered was one of desperate unhappiness.

Lucy was illegitimate and her mother was a remarkably insensitive woman who, from the child's earliest days, lost no opportunity of reminding her that she was a 'nuisance' and had 'ruined her mother's life'.

When Lucy was two, her stepfather deserted her mother. Seen from a child's point of view, of course, the man did not desert the mother — he deserted Lucy. In term's of the child's instinctive logic, the father figure had rejected *her*. The father figure could not be wrong, therefore he had done the right thing in rejecting her. Therefore, if she could not be good enough to keep her own father, she could not be worthy of anyone else's continuing affection.

When Lucy was four, her mother suffered from an extreme case of neurotic depression and at one point even tried to suffocate the child with a pillow. Fortunately she did not carry the deed through, and Lucy woke up as though from a bad dream.

The mother's conscience plagued her, however, and when Lucy was in her teens, her mother confessed to her what she had tried to do.

Now Lucy felt rejected, not only by her father who had abandoned her, but by her mother, who had thought her so unworthy that she had actually tried to kill her.

From that time onwards, Lucy was a person adrift on the sea of life. Although she was exceptionally pretty, bright and intelligent, she had no sense of direction or security. She went from man to man. Though many of these men were genuinely fond of her, Lucy's belief in her own unworthiness was such that she perversely anticipated their ultimate disapproval of her by breaking off the relationships herself.

The best thing that ever happened to her was to meet Gerry — a perceptive and understanding young man.

Now, in the ultimate irony, she had brought Gerry to see us for treatment of *his* alleged mental disability.

In order to set Lucy back on the path to happiness and a mature understanding of life, it was necessary to adjust her Inner Face.

She and her husband both showed a quick appreciation of Hypnothink and Gerry proved of great assistance to his wife in her adjustment to the techniques of improvement.

In the early stages we struck an unexpected snag.

Lucy was advised to think back upon her life and seize upon any exceptionally happy experience, focus upon the emotional sensation and cultivate it.

Lucy had pathetically few happy moments to recall. The one she chose was her memory of walking in a street, with her husband holding her hand.

She was asked to build upon this memory of contentment and to construct an enduring attitude of serenity using the memory as a basis.

But she soon reported that, whenever she ventured to relive this moment of happiness, her thoughts took her relentlessly on to the unhappy conclusion — which, of course, she had not mentioned previously.

It seemed that Gerry had discontinued the practice of walking hand-in-hand with his wife in the street because he had somehow been persuaded that this was not a 'contemporary' thing to do.

To someone of Lucy's vulnerability, this action — which she saw as a withdrawal of affection — by her husband had been extremely wounding. In her own words, it was like 'a dagger being twisted in my heart'.

No matter how she tried, Lucy could not recall the good part on its own. Always it led on to what she called 'the knife'.

Finally we found another happy image of her sadly depleted rag-bag of memories. It was a moment of safety — sitting on the floor, watching television, leaning back against her husband's legs as he sat in his favourite chair.

Lucy was able to retain this image of happiness and reproduce the mood it generated. Gradually, and with practice, she cultivated and maintained an attitude of serenity which is still with her. Her savage bouts of unfounded jealousy are now well and truly in the past.

Lucy and Gerry have a sound marriage.

12.

'I Don't Like Flowers'

Connie Dexter turned the bacon on the grill until the slices were exactly the way her husband John liked them — slightly crisp and turning up at the edges. Two fried eggs, a slice of fried bread and a big pot of coffee. She loved to see John attack a meal with gusto. She assembled everything on a tray and took it through to the breakfast room and slipped the plate onto the table in front of John. He smiled at her and began to eat.

Connie thought again how extraordinarily like Steve McQueen her husband looked. He had the same compact look, the same tight curly fair hair, the same clear blue eyes.

She knew that she could count herself lucky that he was such a good husband and father.

Mara, their three-year-old daughter sat quietly toying with her food.

John finished his breakfast, drank his coffee, looked up at the kitchen clock and saw that he had exactly fifteen minutes in which to get to work. The office was only a short distance away so he would make it in comfortable time.

John slipped on his jacket, kissed Connie affectionately and tousled his little daughter's hair on his way out.

Connie waved to him from the door of the breakfast room and he waved back. He opened the front door and stepped through.

Once outside, he did a strange thing. Hastily he shut the door behind him and, grasping the handle, he turned his face to the door as though he were about to re-enter the house. His eyes were squeezed shut and the bones of his knuckles showed white through the skin of his clenched fists.

John Dexter was terrified.

Gradually the first awful, consuming fear subsided and the trembling of his limbs began to abate. He felt as though he were about to faint and the noise of the traffic echoed distantly somewhere inside his head. But now that he had the first terror under control, he turned away from the door and prepared to face the world.

Slowly he walked away from his home, one reluctant step following another as he forced himself to go to work, away from the sanctuary of his own home — out into the awful, threatening, consuming world.

With an ability born of long practice, John Dexter was able to force a faint smile onto his lips and he glanced casually about him, as though he were feeling nonchalant and at ease — just another businessman strolling slowly to work.

But every step was a distillation of anxiety. Unspoken horrors were everywhere about him. Unexpected menaces lay in wait around every corner. When he reached the park which stretched out on his left, Dexter reeled slightly from an intensification of anguish. Open spaces were a particular threat to his peace of mind.

Thank God, he thought, he had only another three blocks to go. On he trudged, conquering his fear every second only to have it attack him again immediately.

If only, he thought desperately — if only he had a friend waiting in a parked car a hundred yards further up the road — a car with the engine on, the motor running and the door half-open, so that he could leap inside and escape.

Beads of chill perspiration had formed on his forehead by this time. Dexter knew from experience that the cold fringe along his hairline indicated that he only had a few more seconds of exposure before he was within the gates of the firm where he worked. At least there he would be comparatively safe — haunted only by the terrifying thought of the journey home again.

He went through the gates and into the building where he spent his days. He sat down tremulously and tried not to think of the ordeal he had just experienced. Gradually his composure returned. At least he was safe here until five o'clock. He picked up the morning paper and tried to concentrate on the day's news.

At eleven o'clock that morning, John Dexter received a message that the works foreman would like to see him. John finished his mug of coffee and walked across to the foreman's office.

'Morning,' said Thompson, the foreman.

'Morning,' replied Dexter. He liked Thompson, a big bluff man.

'We've got a bit of a problem, John,' said the foreman. 'And you're the one who can solve it for us.'

'What do you mean?' asked Dexter, puzzled.

'Nobody over at Upham seems to have the faintest notion of how to handle the new machine,' said Thompson. 'You know, the Goliath 4000.'

Dexter grinned. 'Oh well, they can be temperamental.'

'Just so,' said Thompson. 'Not to beat about the bush, John, they're so desperate over there that they've asked me to send them someone to run the machine for the next three months and give them some idea of how to keep it going smoothly after that.' He paused, and lit a cigarette. 'So I'm afraid you're it. You're the only man with the know-how that I can spare.'

John Dexter looked at the foreman in awed silence as comprehension came to him. Thompson was sending him to Upham to run the Goliath. But Upham was twelve miles away . . .

'Upham is twelve miles away,' he said limply, his words reflecting the thought which overshadowed his mind.

'Don't worry, lad,' said Thompson, grinning. 'You'll get expenses money.'

'But I can't do it,' said Dexter, knowing that he sounded like a fool. He felt strange — disembodied — and he seriously suspected that he was going to faint.

'What do you mean, you can't do it?' said Thompson. He laughed loudly and gave Dexter a playful clout on the arm. 'You've got nothing to complain about man! It'll be like three months holiday. I wish I were in your shoes, I can tell you.' He turned his mind to other matters. 'Right, that's settled then. You're at Upham from Monday.' He picked up the phone.

Dexter turned and walked away. His fragile serenity had been shattered.

I can't go to Upham, he thought hopelessly. I can hardly negotiate the six blocks from my house in the morning. How on earth can I make it all the way to the railway station and then go another twelve miles on the train. And once I'm on the train, I won't be able to get out between stations.

The thought triggered another wave of dread. John began to feel physically ill. He sat down heavily and tried to think of some way out.

He could pretend he was ill, of course. But that wasn't really any kind of solution. He couldn't keep it up for three months. And anyway, he couldn't fool Connie that he was sick when he wasn't. He had tried that game before, when the thought of going to work had become too much for him. He could get away with a day or two at home, but no more.

What made the whole thing worse was that he was conscientious about his work and he knew that he could do this particular job — and do it well. The people at Upham would be counting on him. Plus the fact that he couldn't afford to stay away from work. He needed the money.

By the time John Dexter left work that evening to face the painful walk through those threatening streets on the way home, his mood was almost suicidal.

But, by the rules he had laid down for himself, he couldn't tell a soul in the world about his dilemma. His wife didn't even suspect that he only felt safe and unthreatened when he was safely in his own home. She had no inkling that he had to summon up every scrap of his considerable courage just to walk across a road. She didn't know that, every time he had to pass an open space, her husband seriously feared that he would actually lose consciousness.

How could he tell Connie, now, at this stage in their marriage, that he had these strange fears. He couldn't even explain them to himself. He just knew that he experienced them and that, for the past few months, they had been getting worse and worse.

Dexter reached his front door at last and, as he did every day when he returned from work, he paused, took out his handkerchief, and wiped the sweat of fear from his forehead. Then, with a deep breath, he composed his features and walked into the house with a smile on his face.

Connie met him with a hug and a kiss. She was cheerful and full of news — what Mara had done that day — what the neighbours had been up to.

She made her husband a pot of tea and Dexter allowed himself to savour the beautiful, wonderful sensation of being able to relax completely for the first time since he had walked out of the front door that morning.

After they had eaten and Mara was asleep, John and his wife settled down in front of the television.

'Have you anything in mind for next Sunday, John?' she asked as she put a cup of coffee on the small table beside him.

'I don't think so,' he said. 'Why, what's so special about next Sunday?'

'It's your birthday, that's what!' said Connie smiling.

'So it is,' said John. 'I'd forgotten all about it.'

'I thought we could take Mara and go to see the ornamental gardens,' said Connie. 'After all, she's old enough to appreciate them now. And you know how much I want to see them. The closest we've ever got to them was that programme on the telly last year.'

'No, Connie,' said John brusquely. 'You know I don't like flowers. They give me hay-fever.'

'But it seems so silly, not going to the gardens when they're so close by — right on our doorstep really. It's only four miles, after all. And we could take a picnic lunch and have a lovely day.'

'I said no,' said Dexter. His voice was uncustomarily harsh.

Connie looked at her husband with surprise. He could be so stubborn and unreasonable sometimes.

Connie was a tolerant and easy-going woman — a pretty, young wife who was perfectly happy with her life as a wife and mother. She asked nothing of her husband other than his continued presence and love. But even she felt a surge of annoyance now.

'Oh, really John!' She put down her tea-cup with a bang. 'I've been trying to get you to take us to the gardens for nearly two years now. Don't you think that's a ridiculous situation? I've a good mind to take Mara on my own!'

For Connie, this was real rebellion. John looked at her, startled by the flash of temper. Without a word, he got up and walked into the bedroom, closing the door behind him.

He sat on the bed, close to total despair.

What kind of man am I? he thought hopelessly. What a pathetic excuse for a husband and father! I can't even take my wife and child to visit a public flower garden — all because I'm terrified of the journey. What kind of weird ailment is this? I must be going mad!

That thought had occurred to him before, more than once, when he had realized the impossibility of explaining to his friends the extraordinary nature of the fears and anxieties which beset him.

Once he had actually tried to tell someone about it. Celia, his girlfriend at the time, the only girl apart from Connie that he had ever taken out, had listened incredulously as he blurted out the torments which beset him.

He knew at once that he had made an awful mistake. Celia recoiled from him, as though he had some hideous disease. She had refused to see him after that.

That was why he had never told Connie about his 'problem' — as he called it in his own mind. He was afraid that he would lose her. And now his 'problem' seemed to be getting worse instead of going away, as he had hoped it might after getting married.

He felt the intense need to tell someone. Anyone. What a blessed relief it would be to talk honestly and without reserve about the unspeakable horrors he experienced every time he went through his own front door.

Perhaps he could find some way of earning his living at home. Once again, this was a possible avenue of escape he had thought about many times before. But he didn't have that sort of skill. He was strictly the sort of worker who could function well among machines, having been shown exactly what to do.

Despair overcame him.

John Dexter began to think about suicide. Perhaps that would be the best course of action. He would end it all. He had insurance — that would take care of Connie and Mara. Connie was young enough and attractive enough to make a new life for herself. Mara was so young that she would probably forget him altogether in time.

'John!'

He heard Connie's voice.

'John — there's something good on the box. Come on!'

Thank goodness, she was her old sunny self once more. Perhaps she would forget all about the visit to the gardens.

John emerged from the bedroom and sat himself in his favourite chair.

On the television an interviewer was talking to Romark, the hypnotherapist.

Dexter didn't know it at the time, but that was the turning point in his life . . .

Hypnothink in Action

John Dexter came to see me the next day. I had been speaking in the television interview about the therapeutic use of hypnosis — and John had seen in this some hope for his condition.

In his naive ignorance, John had not realized that he suffered, along with many thousands of other people, from agoraphobia — albeit in an extreme form. He was also quite lacking in confidence.

At our first meeting I asked him to describe himself. He said he was 'frightened to go anywhere'. He also insisted that he was 'as thick as two planks'.

I introduced him to the principles of Hypnothink. He was quick to accommodate the theory and was eager to be responsive and co-operative. After all, he had the best of motivations — this was Saturday, and on the Monday morning John Dexter was supposed to undertake the most terrifying expedition of his life — twelve miles by train to a strange town.

It was clear that the first requirement was to adjust John's Inner Face and 'tune' his personality to a mood of some self-esteem.

Accordingly, I asked him to think back on any moment of success he had experienced in his past, to focus upon that emotion and to build upon that basis.

John Dexter sat with me and thought with determination back across his twenty-four years. A look of embarrassment and shame crept across his features.

He could not bring to mind one moment of success in his entire life. Not one fleeting second of pride, of delight in some personal accomplishment.

It was an astonishing, and pathetic, situation.

This was an appropriate occasion for the use of hypnotism. Dexter proved to be a good subject and in a short while I had placed him in an hypnotic trance.

The human mind is like a cine camera which records every sight and every sound during every waking moment. Then the conscious mind intrudes and, for a variety of reasons, it blurs or erases certain memories. Through the use of hypnotism, however, we can reach the subconscious mind — the area of the mind which never forgets.

Patiently I took John Dexter back through his life, month after month, week after week, day after day, right back through the years.

Eventually I began to think that perhaps Dexter was right. That his life did not include one proud moment, one experience he could use as a basic building block for a structure of confidence.

Fifteen years of age, fourteen, thirteen, twelve, eleven, ten . . . still nothing of consequence.

It was as though John Dexter was a clean slate upon which success had never left the slightest trace or mark. I began to feel despair, but continued to regress him.

Nine years old, eight years old — suddenly we had it! In the childish voice of an eight-year-old, Dexter told me that he had been playing football for the third form that day and he had scored a goal — the only goal of the match — against the second form who were much bigger and older boys.

All his schoolfriends had slapped him on the back and told him what a terrific fellow he was.

'How do you feel?' I asked.

'I feel proud of myself,' said the 'child' — the high, piping voice emanating strangely from John Dexter's adult form.

Before wakening him from his trance, I instructed him that he would retain a full and clear memory of the incident when he awoke. This he did.

On that flimsy basis we set out to reconstruct John Dexter's life.

The transition was swift and profound.

He began a course of treatment in which he would think through that scene on the school soccer field some fifteen years previously and savour the essence of his emotions after receiving praise for his goal. He was to rethink it frequently — at every possible moment during the day — while he was at work or at home. And he was to make a special point of reliving the experience every night in bed before he went to sleep. Slowly he was to build up a deposit of confidence and self-esteem.

It was just one week later — the following Saturday — that John Dexter came to see me again. The first time he came to me, he had sidled apologetically through the door, eyes downcast.

Now he strode through the door with his hand outstretched. He seized my hand in a confident grip and pumped it up and down.

His comment was to the point: 'We've done it!'

He explained that he had gained benefit from the treatment at once. He had been able to make the train journey to his new place of work on the Monday. What is more, they were so pleased with him there that they were already talking of promoting him.

John told me all about his wife's wish to visit the ornamental flower gardens and how, up to now, he had been avoiding the issue.

'I've arranged to take them there on Monday, which is a public holiday,' he told me smiling. 'After all, what's four miles to a seasoned traveller like me? I've been going twelve miles a day to work and twelve miles back.'

John was actually looking forward with eager anticipation to the visit and was confident that he and his family would have an enjoyable time. There wasn't one negative thought on the horizon of his mind. The transition was remarkable.

But he had saved the best news for last.

John had made a crucial breakthrough, all on his own, during that momentous week. Constantly thinking back on his success on the soccer field had made him inquisitive about the game, and he had plucked up enough courage to go down to the village green one afternoon when the local amateur side was practising. He asked if he could join in — and he found, to his surprise, that he had a natural flair for the game.

'It's ridiculously easy for me,' he told me. 'I'm the best player there, even though I'm not a hundred per cent fit. But once I have the ball I know that none of them can take it away from me.'

At the age of twenty-four John Dexter had discovered that he was a natural athlete. Now his life had the vital focus so necessary for the maintenance of his self-esteem and the building of his confidence. Events in his younger life, such as his parents moving home constantly, had contrived to keep him from successful participation in sports. His gnawing insecurities had only served to increase his agoraphobia. But that was all in the past now. In one week, he had been cured of his agoraphobia and his life-path had been diverted from disaster to success.

The fact that football had become a lifeline for John Dexter was no more than a fluke. If the process of hypnotic regression had uncovered some other positive aspect of his life at the age of eight — for instance, if he had made a toy for himself and had been praised for it — it would have been just as possible for us to build upon *that* fact. And then John Dexter might have found his personal salvation as an inventor . . .

13.

The Furniture Mover

Tom Pryor worked the lather to a foaming head on the shaving stick and tilted his cheek as he applied the soap. As he shaved, he thought back over the events of the weekend. He felt quick concern mingled with annoyance as he remembered Saturday night. He and his wife, Robyn, had been invited to a friend's home at the coast. Because of problems at work, Tom had not been able to get away until the Saturday.

Once they had been installed in their room, Robyn had started on about the furniture again.

It would actually be quite funny if it weren't so bloody annoying, he thought ruefully. Obsessive behaviour, that's what it was.

Every time Robyn found herself in a new room, she had this compulsion to move the furniture around. Not just a mild adjustment of position, either. She wanted to shift everything about completely.

He had avoided the issue on Saturday night by applying a firm hand to Robyn's elbow and steering her straight downstairs to join the others. And he had been heavy-handed in pouring her drinks, so that she had had no trouble in falling asleep.

But he had awakened at five the next morning to the sound of Robyn grunting with exertion as she shifted the heavy wardrobe from the position in the corner of the room that it had occupied for years.

Tom tilted his head back to shave the tricky angles around his chin and a ray of early morning sunlight fell across his eyes. The mirror showed him his face unflatteringly in the hard light.

Tom put down the razor and gazed at himself.

Last night, just before they had left John's home for the drive back to London, John's wife had produced an old photograph album.

'I thought you might find these amusing,' she had said, opening the battered album to a double spread of photographs tinged with yellow.

They were pictures he and John had quite forgotten about. Taken some twenty years before, they showed the old friends in almost alien surroundings, their hair incredible short, the women oddly dressed — and all of them quite remarkably slender.

The sight of those forgotten photos had sent a pang of inexplicable anguish through him. Perhaps it was simply the pain of nostalgia — a sorrow at times past, never to be regained.

Tom looked at his features in the shaving mirror, remembering how he had appeared in the snapshots. Now his hair was much more sparse and there was a subtle change in the configuration of his face.

He felt a sense of disquietude flood through him.

Hastily he finished shaving and went down to breakfast. Robyn was seated at the table, buttering her toast.

They ate quietly, saying little. They were both people who took time to 'come to' in the mornings and they had long since discovered that monosyllables were the best marital policy for them at this hour.

Robyn was thirty. She had vivid blue eyes, dark brown hair and a creamy complexion. She was a beauty by any standards and he appreciated her.

Even now, at the breakfast table, she had taken the trouble to groom herself. She looked immaculate. The recognition of this fact made him feel even more unsettled, although he could not have explained why.

'I shan't be home before seven tonight,' he said, rising from the table. 'Something left over from Friday.'

He bent over to kiss his wife on the forehead. She smiled up at him. As he turned to walk away, she stood up with a restraining hand. She plucked a few strands of hair from his shoulder.

'I think you're going a wee bit bald, my darling,' she said lightly.

Tom said nothing, but felt a sharp jab of rage. He opened the door and strode out without looking back. Next month I'll be forty-two, he thought grimly.

After her husband had gone, Robyn went back to her dressing table and restored the make-up which had been mildly damaged by the act of eating.

She studied herself closely. Her hair was its natural colour, even to the occasional traces of grey, which fortunately were so light that they suggested that highlights had been applied to the hair. Every second office girl seemed to have highlights these days, she thought with disapproval. All those female lemmings, hurrying to hurl themselves over the cliff of conformity.

At least she looked like herself and defiantly so.

Robyn set out on her four-block walk to the bus stop. Going to work by bus in the morning took twice as long, but everyone went by tube and she hated the prospect of being crammed in those cheerless carriages like a commuting sardine. And anyway, from the bus she could at least look out at the passing parade.

Robyn had been with the same firm for eight years. At first she had been a shorthand typist, but had soon worked her way up and become personal secretary to the managing director. A few years ago she had persuaded him to make her the company's press liaison officer.

The job was an important one, although by its nature it kept her busy only in sporadic bursts during the year But she was the only PRO on the staff, and that pleased her.

As she sat in the bus, skimming through the paper, she remembered that night at John's house in the guest room.

Worry etched lines on her forehead. That damned furniture. It had looked so — so *stereotyped*, somehow. As though a situation was being forced upon her — a situation she *had* to accept.

Tom just could not understand what it was that made her move the furniture about. And yet it was so obvious. She was simply imposing their own ambiance on their surroundings. What could be more logical than that?

She thought back to how it all began. It was many years ago, when she had been working in Birmingham, and her firm had sent her on a series of weekly visits to London. They had booked her into the Regent Palace Hotel in Piccadilly Circus.

She stayed there for three consecutive weeks. That was how she discovered that the rooms were all identical. And that was when, in an outburst of individualism, she had moved the furniture about to make her room unique in that monument to conformity.

After that, whenever she stayed in a hotel, she found it necessary to change the furniture arrangement. And now, in recent years, the compulsion came upon her in private homes as well.

But the basic principle remained valid. Why should she have to be in the same surroundings as everyone else?

Yet the worry remained. It was a pity that Tom couldn't see it from her point of view . . .

Tom left his office in the insurance company early that evening and went to a pub in Hampstead which he hadn't visited in months. That particular evening he felt the need to cut himself off from his familiar cronies, to strike out on his own.

The pub had a long bar with high stools. He chose one in an unoccupied stretch and ordered a drink. It was the sort of pub which drew tourists as well as regulars from the area, and it had an unusually high proportion of good-looking girls, many of them visitors to London.

Tom looked about him, sizing up the girls. He felt a trifle daring — irresponsible, uncaring — even dashing. The thought made him a little embarrassed, as though he had said the words out loud. He turned to order another drink and, as the barman prepared it for him, he saw in the mirror a young girl approaching. She had short blonde hair with a tousled look. She sat down next to him, put her handbag on the counter and began to rummage through it.

The girl seemed friendly and open and, to Tom's surprise, within minutes he had bought her a drink and they were chatting as though they were old friends. He couldn't remember the last time he had spoken to a strange woman in a pub.

The girl was a Scot and her accent had a pleasant, soft sound. She explained that she was down from Edinburgh to visit her uncle. She had only just arrived, but her uncle wasn't at home so she had come round to the pub for a drink and to kill time.

She was twenty-one and her name was Kathy.

When Kathy mentioned her age, Tom glanced involuntarily in the mirror above the bar. They looked like father and daughter, he thought grimly. But Kathy didn't seem to mind. She was laughing, gay and vivacious.

He could swear that she was flirting with him. She laughed at everything he said and she was glancing up at him coquettishly.

The presence of this vibrant young woman next to him, hanging on his every word, gave Tom a sense of heady elation. Then he realized the time. It was seven-thirty. He had said that he would be home by seven!

The realization snapped him out of his happy mood. He felt sober and cast down. 'I must go,' he said curtly. 'I hadn't realized how late it was.'

Kathy looked disappointed. 'Please don't go just yet,' she said, with a candour which he found disarming. 'You're the only friend I have in England.' She said it flippantly, but he sensed a need in her words.

'I really must go,' he said. 'But perhaps we can meet again.'

'I'll be here at the same time tomorrow,' said Kathy. When he got to the door, he looked back and she was still looking at him. She smiled and waved her hand.

As he drove home, Tom felt more cheerful than he had for months.

Robyn didn't question him about being late. She was watching television. They had a late dinner and went to bed.

During the following fortnight Tom got to know Kathy very well. He met her every second or third night, and she was always so cheerful and just as attentive a listener as she had been on that first chance meeting.

At first Tom found Kathy's enthusiasm for him a bewildering experience. It confronted him with a ticklish decision — or so he thought. How was he supposed to behave towards this young girl? Did she expect him to be avuncluar and nothing more?

He was afraid to overstep the mark. He couldn't visualize anything more humiliating than to be rebuffed by this youngster and accused of being a middle-aged oaf.

But it soon became obvious that Kathy had no such reservations about their relationship. She became openly affectionate, holding his hand at the bar and even kissing him goodnight.

She treated him almost like an oracle, he thought with mild amusement as he drove home for the weekend. Every opinion he proffered was received with respect, as though she was very much aware that he was a man of experience. And what a lovely sense of humour she had!

She made no bones about wanting to see him as often as possible. She had even invited him round this weekend. Her uncle had to leave London for four days and she had the place to herself. Excitement quickened within him at the thought.

She had written the address and telephone number on a card and given it to him.

'Come if you can,' she had said with her quicksilver laugh. 'I'm not going anywhere.' Then she was suddenly serious. 'I only have another two weeks in London, you know. Then it's back home again.'

I'm actually considering going to bed with this girl, thought Tom in amazement as he turned the car into the driveway of his home. I'm forty-one — well, almost forty-two — and I'm seriously thinking of slipping off for a dirty weekend with a kid of twenty-one.

What has happened to me? He pulled the car to a halt and took the keys from the ignition. His hands were shaking. He felt as guilty as a thief.

He sat in the car for a full five minutes, trying to compose himself. Then he went inside, whistling softly.

Robyn came bustling out of the kitchen to kiss him. 'You are in a cheerful mood tonight,' she said, pecking him on the cheek. Tom stared at her defensively, but she hadn't noticed anything. She didn't even really look at him. She was more concerned with the late edition of the paper he was carrying under his arm.

'Thanks', she said and settled herself in her armchair. 'I'm just going to do the crossword and then we can eat. Do you want to help me?'

Without even looking for a sign of assent from him, she made room for him beside her.

As Tom sat next to his beautiful wife and nodded agreement as she efficiently filled in the crossword, he thought wryly to himself: she takes me for granted. She thinks she knows my every move — my every thought. The idea made him resentful.

After lunch on Sunday, Robyn said she thought she would take the car and go round to her sister's place if Tom didn't mind. Tom said that he had some reading to catch up on and then he might go for a long walk around the common. Robyn said that she would be back by seven and then they could go down to the pub for a few drinks.

Tom tried unsuccessfully for thirty minutes to concentrate on the Sunday papers. Then he gave up. He took out Kathy's card and dialled the number. She was in. She urged him to come round.

By three-thirty Tom was with Kathy. By four o'clock they were in bed together. They made love with sweaty fervour and then sat, naked, drinking red wine. Tom felt like a college boy again.

By seven o'clock Tom was home.

Robyn came back at seven-thirty and together they went down to their local pub for a few Sunday evening drinks. Tom was consumed with guilt and remorse, and he offered her cigarettes, opened doors for her, poured her drinks, kissed her cheek and generally fussed over her in a manner to which she had become totally unaccustomed. She wondered . . .

That evening, after they had drunk a little too much and made love sleepily, Robyn stayed awake for a long, long time.

I wonder if Tom is seeing another woman, she thought. She propped herself up on one elbow and looked at her husband sprawled out next to her on the bed. Asleep and dishevelled, he looked younger and more vulnerable.

Don't tell me, she thought, that I've become just one more cuckolded wife, one of the faceless millions of taken-for-granted wives.

The thought gnawed at her self-esteem and kept her awake for hours.

Tom paid the taxi-driver and strode eagerly towards the pub. For the past few days he had been unusually busy and he hadn't been able to get away to see Kathy at all. It was her last week in London and she had phoned him at the office to tell him how much she was missing him.

The past fortnight had been a difficult time for Tom. His developing romance with young Kathy had sent him into an emotional turmoil which he didn't fully understand.

For a time he had thought that Robyn might suspect the truth. On impulse he had bought a complete outfit of new clothes and Robyn had ventured the opinion that perhaps they were a bit 'young' for him. Then, after a speculative pause, she said: 'What's come over you Tom? There's something about you . . .

And she began to question his movements.

Previously she had hardly seemed to notice whether he was home early or late. At one time he had regarded this good-natured acceptance of his habitual unpunctuality as a minor virtue. Now he was put out that she should be so conscious of his time-keeping.

But somehow he had managed to divert her questions. And he always made a point of being especially attentive to her needs when he was with her.

But now, at last, he had arranged to have the entire evening free. He could focus his attention on Kathy without having to watch the clock.

He went straight to the bar counter. Kathy was not there yet. The barman, serving a couple some distance away, saw him and smiled a greeting.

Then he came across and handed Tom a letter: 'Dearest Tom — just a hurried note to explain that Uncle Charles is driving up to Edinburgh this afternoon and has offered to take me — so I shan't be able to see you this evening. Sorry — but I'm sure you'll understand. It's been lots of fun knowing you — love, Kathy.'

He looked up and saw the barman's enquiring gaze.

'Yes, of course, a whisky please.'

So Kathy had gone out of his life as effortlessly as she had entered it.

He sat sipping his drink. 'Lots of fun!' So that was what Kathy felt about him. She made it sound like a trip to a fun fair!

It suddenly struck him just how important this young girl had become in his life. In his assessment of personal priorities, Kathy came first as his principal source of pleasure and everything else had been secondary. No, that wasn't quite true. *Robyn* was first in his scale of values. But Kathy had been different — outside the normal boundaries of his life. Different — and important.

And now she had gone. Tom looked around the bar, filling up now as people arrived from the city.

Two drinks later he struck up a conversation with a rather plain girl from Australia who introduced him to her party of friends. Among them was a 25-year-old researcher with an advertising agency — a girl with huge, brown eyes and a slight lisp. Her name was Maureen and she was married to a copy-writer — and he discovered later that evening, back at an account executive's flat, that she was a sexual predator.

They began to meet for lunch at the flat of one of her girlfriends. It was only two blocks away from Maureen's office and Tom, for the first time in twenty years, began to have sexual adventures at a time when he would normally have been downing a pint and a sandwich.

Maureen had a slightly gushing enthusiasm which made her appear to hang on his every word. She would gaze up at him with wide-eyed adoration and say things like: 'I like older men — they're

so worldly and confident,' and 'I defy any man under thirty-five
to be truly debonair . . .'

She was a perceptive woman beneath that attitude of helpless
vulnerability, he thought.

It never seemed to bother her that he was married. Come to that,
he thought sardonically, it didn't seem to bother her that *she* was
married.

Maureen amused him and flattered him with her attention. But
she had small mannerisms which began to irritate him.

One Thursday, when they had both taken the afternoon off, and
spent it in bed together, he was lying back quietly and contempla-
tively when Maureen came back from the bathroom and sat down
next to him in her impetuous way.

'Why do you do this, Tom?' she asked.

'What do you mean?' he said, a trifle testily.

'This. Making love to me. Just look at your face. You look so
utterly unhappy. Why come here with me if it's going to make you
sad?'

He felt himself colour with a mixture of embarrassment and
anger. He *had* been feeling depressed — there was no denying that.
Guilty, actually. But Maureen didn't have to blurt it out so damned
bluntly. That was the trouble with the girl. She had no tact or finesse.

Tom got out of bed and got dressed. With a considerable effort
he retained his normal attitude of nonchalance and unfailing
courtesy. He gave Maureen a farewell kiss. But he felt so relieved
once he was out in the hustle and bustle of the London streets.

He wouldn't see Maureen again. She was a silly little thing
anyway.

A week later Tom went to a sales convention where he was
introduced to a young red-head by the name of Sarah. She worked
for a wine company as a publicist. He took her home that night
and, although they didn't in fact go to bed together, they did go
in for some heavy necking.

When he got home that night Robyn was awake. She found a
trace of lipstick on his shirt collar and claimed that he 'stank like
an Egyptian whorehouse.'

He slumped on the edge of the bed, too tired to argue or pretend.
She accused him of going with other women — of making a mockery
of their marriage.

Self-contempt welled up within him. Everything Robyn was saying was true, and he was too honest a man to deny it — even to himself.

As she saw her husband there, dejected and deflated, his head between his hands, Robyn's rage flamed to a new peak.

He was so brazen about it. He couldn't even be bothered to put up a front — to pretend. He carried on as though she were of no importance at all in his life. She was just another abandoned wife — a domestic chattel.

Suddenly Robyn's anger transmuted itself into grief and she fell across the bed, sobbing desperately.

Tom slowly aroused himself, turned and put his arms around his wife. They stayed like that for a long time, linked by their mutual unhappiness.

Eventually they fell asleep. Tom was the first to wake and he lay silently for a while, remembering the events of the night before.

As he looked down at Robyn asleep next to him, he was tortured by his own conscience. How on earth did he manage to drift into those idiotic affairs with bird-brained girls half his age? His own emotional processes had become a bewildering maelstrom in which he could find no logic. What was he looking for in these liaisons? It wasn't even as though he and Robyn had an unsatisfactory sex life. On the contrary, they had always been unusually well attuned in their sensual appetites.

He decided that he would have to put their relationship back on a proper footing. Of course, he could never tell her about all those other affairs — he would simply admit to having a bit too much to drink and kissing that red-head who had thrown herself at him at the party.

Tom woke Robyn gently. At first she was coldly withdrawn but, as he spoke to her, telling her that she was drawing grossly exaggerated conclusions from a trifling incident, she began to soften.

They decided to go away together for a few days — away from the familiar patterns of their day-to-day behaviour and the irritations of office routine.

They booked into a small hotel in Wales where they had once spent a gloriously sensual weekend. Tom drove there at a leisurely pace which allowed them to enjoy the countryside as they went.

They checked into the hotel at six o'clock, made love unhurriedly and with great relish and had a huge dinner.

They were in bed and asleep by eleven o'clock.

A long time later Tom woke up. He could hear a strange creaking and thumping and sleepily he propped himself up in bed and peered about him.

The room was in complete disarray. Robyn had taken all the smaller articles of furniture and shoved them together in one corner. Now she was pushing the heavy old chest of drawers across the carpet, but one leg had caught the edge of the carpet and she could not budge it.

The light coming through the fanlight fell upon his wife's face. There was perspiration on her forehead and her throat was contorted from the physical effort she was exerting in her desperate attempt to move the heavy piece of furniture. Her eyes had a slightly glazed expression and she reminded him horrifyingly of the face of an Indian mystic he had seen on television a few weeks previously walking across a bed of hot coals.

Tom leaped out of bed. 'For God's sake,' he cried. 'What are you doing?' He shook his wife by the shoulders and slowly her eyes turned towards him.

'I've got to move the furniture,' she said slowly.

'But why?' he demanded. 'What for? It's perfectly all right where it is. It's been there for donkey's years. Why move it around now? What's the point?'

He realized that he was still shaking her. Her head lolled back and forth on her shoulders. She seemed to be in a trance.

'But it's so obvious,' she said. 'We've got to change it. Every other room in this hotel is exactly like this one. The wardrobe is in exactly the same place; the chairs are in the same place; the beds are in the same place . . .' Her voice began to rise like a priest incanting a ritual.

'Stop it, Robyn,' Tom shouted. He took her by the hand and led her to the bed. 'Sit down.' She sat down meekly, like a small child.

'This is becoming more than just an eccentric preoccupation,' he said. 'At first I thought it was a natural feminine thing, to want to move the futniture around a bit whenever we found ourselves in a strange place. But lately it's become much more than that. What about that weekend we spent at John's place a few months ago? You nearly woke everyone up with the noise you were making in the middle of the night. And now this, for God's sake. Look at the time.' He switched on the bedside light. It was 5.15 a.m.

'This whole thing has become an obsession with you and we simply have to do something about it.'

Tom took his wife by the shoulders and turned her to face him. He looked into her face. 'I want you to go for help, Robyn. It's just not normal for a mature woman to be compulsively shifting furniture in the middle of the night.'

Robyn sat silently for a while. Then an emotion he couldn't quite fathom passed across her face.

'All right,' she said quietly. 'I'll go and consult someone. But only if you do too.' She mocked his own words of a moment ago: 'It's just not normal for a mature man to be carrying on with women like a teenager.'

Tom felt a flush spread over his face, but he couldn't quibble now.

'It's arranged then,' he said with all the dignity he could muster. 'Things have been getting a bit out of hand lately. It's about time we put our house in order.'

Hypnothink in Action

A week after the events of which you have just read, Tom and Robyn Prior came to see us.

Robyn thought that her compulsion to shift the hotel furniture came from her sense of rebellion against conformity, that this heightened sense of individualism was a characteristic of her thinking.

But, as usual, the mind was playing tricks, laying false trails, to lead her away from the truth.

Robyn was dissatisfied with her Inner Face.

In a sense she was like the young girl who runs away from home in a small town 'because there are no boys there'. When she gets to the big city she finds that there are no boys there either. Wherever she goes, that girl has the same problem. She is trying to run away from herself.

Robyn was a more sophisticated person than the young girl from the country. But in her Inner Face she was boring and unglamorous. She desired, above all else, to make herself 'special' — different from the common herd.

Robyn's case was something of a rarity in that we had more information than was absolutely necessary to be able to effect a change for the better. More often than not, a therapist has to function on the minimum of essential information.

Because of the effectiveness of the techniques of Hypnothink, it would have been quite possible to treat Robyn on a fairly superficial level only — to imbue her mind's eye with a vivid picture of her arriving at a new residence (whether a hotel or a private home), going to sleep contentedly and waking in the morning in a mood of complete satisfaction with her surroundings.

This would have been enough to eliminate the dissatisfaction which compelled her to move furniture about.

But, being armed with fuller knowledge, it was possible to help Robyn to use Hypnothink in a more intensive way. We were about to reshape her personality and create a new Inner Face based on her sense of individuality — using as a corner-stone the unusual nature of her job as PRO for her firm.

Tom, the husband, had a problem which was in many ways similar to that which bedevilled his wife. But it was necessary to use entirely different means to overcome it.

He was a less magnetic person than she. He had an Inner Face of only mediocre quality — and it had never changed. Although he was now in his early forties, his Inner Face was virtually the same as it had been twenty years ago.

Quite understandably, Tom became bored with himself. His disenchantment was made more hurtful by the knowledge that the passage of time was eroding his looks.

When he looked in the shaving mirror that morning, it was for him a moment of truth. He had to face himself — and he did not like what he saw.

Women in their middle years can boost a flagging ego at times like these by buying a new outfit, or having a new hairdo. A man does not have such a readily accessible solution.

In Tom's case he followed a well-worn path. Like thousands of middle-aged men before him, he sought his lost youth in the arms of younger women.

Tom changed his Inner Face — even though only fleetingly — by seeing himself reflected in the eyes of young girls who thought of him as a sophisticated man, more experienced in the ways of the world. They treated him with respect and were inclined to hang on his every word.

Of course the trouble was that Tom began to expect more from these relationships than they were able, by their very nature, to provide. So the temporary rewards of self-esteem were soon cancelled out by the final cynical realization that these young women had only a transient interest in him.

The girls were a respite from the mediocrity of his life.

Tom proved to be very responsive to Hypnothink, understanding the principles and the implicit common sense of it.

His treatment took the form of a programming in which he adjusted his Inner Face to give himself an image of a man who was attractive to the opposite sex. We soon established this realization — and once he had accepted this as a fact, he no longer had the need to prove himself constantly. He gained the necessary maturity and, in the process, rediscovered the value of his wife as a friend and a sexual partner.

14.

Years in the Rough

Bobby James made his assessment with confident judgement. No wind. The fairway was crisp. About 300 yards to the green.

He was at a crucial stage of the game now. If he won this game, he won the tournament. £5,000! That was more money than he had ever had at any one time. Elation lifted his spirits.

He looked about him once more, head on one side, his muscular frame clad only in the lightest of clothes, leaving his body free for easy movement.

James took his driver and hefted it between his hands. It was a familiar feeling and a pleasing one. Confidence seemed to seep down his arms and right into the club.

Live dangerously! he thought with a mischievous flippancy. Live dangerously — for five thousand quid!

He settled himself, twirled his driver in what seemed to the onlookers to be a frivolous gesture, and then hit the ball with ferocious strength backed up by the most intense concentration he could muster.

He'd hit the ball with the intention of sending it down the fairway like a bullet, to land on the green and roll close up to the flag.

'My God, he's on the green!' Somebody's whispered comment reached his ears and Bobby grinned wolfishly. He strode off, whistling through his teeth.

On the green he saw it was a long putt. Never mind — he could do it.

He bent down and studied the lie of the ball. Then, making his mind up swiftly, he seized the club, twirled it absentmindedly in his hands, and struck the ball. It ran along the green and disappeared into the cup as though it had been pulled in by an invisible string.

Cries of excitement rose from some of the onlookers, followed by the more discreet clapping of the rest of the crowd.

Bobby James had won the tournament with an eagle. It was characteristic of the man, thought the golf correspondent of the *Star,* watching the athlete's face as he smiled and shook hands, that he should win with such flamboyance.

Bobby James was the newest star on the golfing horizon — and one of the brashest. His cock-sure attitude had resulted in the press having a love-hate relationship with him. He was always good for a quote, but his self-assurance often invited criticism.

Jones, the reporter, strolled over to the champion.

'Congratulations Bobby,' he said and shook the man's hand

'Thanks,' said James. 'I had the feeling I'd get an eagle on that last one. Nothing could go wrong for me today.'

'You're certainly on a winning streak right now,' said Jones 'How about a quote from the new champion. To what do you attribute your success?'

Bobby James grinned. 'That's easy. I believe in going for the kill! Never play safe.'

The reporter smiled. He could see the headline already.

'That's great,' he said. 'So, what about the future? Have you made any plans?'

'I'll be playing at every opportunity,' said Bobby. 'I want to play on every course I can, in every country. I want to win them all!' He flung his arms wide in a gesture of youthful enthusiasm.

'You probably will,' said the golfing correspondent. 'You're just the type to do it. Brilliant, tough and ambitious.'

'You've forgotten something,' said Bobby James, his smile broadening.

'What's that?'

'I'm hungry for money! Hungry as hell!'

With that, Bobby James turned and went off to the changing rooms, acknowledging the praise and plaudits from the crowd as he went.

As Bobby James parked his gleaming silver sedan, he suddenly realized what it was that had been gnawing away at the back of his mind from the moment he had got up that morning.

He was back. Back at the course where he'd made his first big killing — exactly seven years ago today!

He got out of the car and stretched in the morning sunshine It was a beautiful course, but he'd played on a hundred better.

He thought back to the wonderful day, seven years ago, when he had clinched his victory with an eagle on the final hole.

He shook his head and grinned to himself. Those were the days, he thought. He just couldn't go wrong in those days. And what's more, he hadn't even been able to envisage the possibility of anything going wrong. The ball was there, he hit it — and it always went just where he wanted it to. He had charmed that ball, just like a witch-doctor throwing bones.

A lot had happened to Bobby James in those seven years. He had won many tournaments in many different parts of the world. He had become a familiar personality on the television screens of many nations. They had watched his triumphs and his tantrums. There were those who admired his flamboyance. Others detested him. But everyone agreed that he played exciting golf.

It hasn't been so exciting lately, Bobby James thought sourly. Still, you couldn't win them all . . .

What the public didn't know was that Bobby James was now a very rich man. He had won a lot of money and he had used it well. He owned tracts of land and property in the most unlikely places. He was financially secure for life — and that was a comforting thought.

As he went into the clubhouse, he thought back on the conversation he had had with his broker just the day before. James had invested heavily in gold shares two years previously, and now he was reaping the benefits.

'You're a born speculator,' the broker had said admiringly. 'I wish I had your prescience.'

It wasn't prescience, it was just luck, thought Bobby. He had played in a tournament in South Africa and he had met a mining tycoon at a party. The man had given him some advice and Bobby had taken it. As a result, his fortune had expanded considerably.

Still, money ceased to have much importance once you had eliminated the need to think about it. But its presence had certainly taken that savage edge of anxiety off his personality.

Bobby greeted the familiar faces — the friends, the semi-enemies, the envious, the ambitious, the glory-seekers. He spoke to a few reporters and television people.

Then he concentrated on his game. He played moderately well, but he didn't feel that tingle of elation — that uplift of confidence — which had improved his game so dramatically that day seven years ago.

Gradually the game resolved itself.

An Australian named Corbett, a wiry young man with wild hair and a temperament to match, had been playing consistently under par and had taken what seemed to be a commanding lead. But then, in a fit of childish pique, he had gone to pieces and now he and Bobby were neck and neck.

Bobby James watched the young man's dazzling temperament with weary amusement. Professional golf soon knocked on the head such luxuries of the ego as excessive temperament. Either you managed to curb it or you inevitably dropped out of serious competition.

Corbett was quiet now, his nostrils pinched with concentration as he addressed himself to the ball. There was a gasp of approval from the crowd as he connected with his driver and the ball swooped upwards in a lazy parabola. It was a magnificent drive, taking the ball well down the fairway to the green nearly 300 yards away.

Patiently Bobby took his turn. Unconsciously he twirled the club in the gesture which had now become his trademark. But it slipped between his fingers which were moist and he suddenly felt ill at ease.

Bobby rearranged his stance and addressed himself to the ball once again. For a moment he felt a spurt of the old recklessness — hit it and don't give a damn! But the feeling passed. He knew that wasn't the right way. He had to play sensibly. He swung back and hit the ball with cool precision, aiming it in the general direction of the green and hoping for the best. It was a competent stroke, but not splendid enough to evoke any reaction from the crowd.

It took him another stroke to get on to the green.

But Corbett had experienced another nervous trauma and Bobby found himself level-pegging once again. And this was the last hole!

Sheer luck had thrown him into a winning situation again. Bobby felt the pressure of decision upon him once more. It had become an unfamiliar sensation in recent months.

If he could sink this putt the match was his. He tried to control the rising gorge of anxiety. What the hell, he thought. It's only a game. And even if I didn't sink it, I'll still be second. And on this course, in this tournament, that carries a prize of £4,000.

The effect of inflation on golf purses, he thought wryly, remembering what a spur the thought of a first prize of £5,000 had been to him in his enthusiasm of seven years ago.

Why on earth was he worrying about the size of the prize money?

He didn't need it. He need never work again if he didn't want to

Feeling devil-may-care, he swung the putter back and forth and then prepared to hit the ball. He noticed that, for some reason, his hands were shaking.

He felt disembodied, like someone watching himself from a distance. The club swung in his hands and connected with the ball. It ran erratically across the grass and came to a stop a good five feet from the pin. There was a slight groan from the crowd. Bobby walked slowly up to the ball and hit it again with a perfunctory, one-handed swing of the putter. The ball rolled on and came to a halt about three inches from the hole. This time the crowd moaned dismally. There were a few whistles of disbelief.

Bobby James knocked the ball in for the three-put. He had blown it! He had played like a rank amateur. He felt ashamed, humiliated.

He walked quickly back to the clubhouse, eyes downcast so that he would not have to meet the unspoken accusation in the eyes of the onlookers.

Six months later Bobby James was feeling as nervous as he could ever remember feeling before. There was a chill wind cutting across the golf course, but he was shivering as much from nerves as from the cold.

He was about to play in an international championship. In his own mind Bobby had decided that this was to be the test. Either he still had what it took or he had lost it. This match would tell him — one way or the other.

As he approached the first tee he saw the overflowing crush of spectators and the television crew. The whole bloody world was watching!

If I don't come up to scratch today, I might as well give up the game for good, he thought bitterly.

He assessed the course once again. There was quite a considerable wind. And there was some unpleasant rough to the left of the fairway. He was frightened of this. If he fell in there he would have a very difficult extricating shot to the green and he didn't want to get off to a bad start.

I'll play it safe, he thought to himself, and use a number two iron. It won't give me the distance, but it'll be more accurate than the driver.

His choice of club caused a little eddy of comment among the onlookers. Bobby ignored them. In earlier days he would have grinned defiantly at them, perhaps flourishing his club. Now he pretended not to hear.

He swung the club a few times and then twirled it in an attempt at nonchalance. But, again, the club slipped in his hands. He felt angry and upset for no real reason. He grabbed the club firmly, addressed himself to the ball and swung. He connected with more power than he had intended.

As he watched the flight of the ball, he realized that he had used too much right hand. The ball had been well struck, but hooked, and it flighted to the left, falling in the thickest part of the rough.

It was fully 200 yards from the green.

As Bobby James trudged along towards the ball, his mind was a confusion of impressions. I'm in trouble already, he thought with a blind despair. I should have used the driver after all. He refused to look to either side, but he could feel the eyes of the crowd upon him. He could just imagine the comments of the television commentator to all those millions of watching people.

His caddy guided him to the ball and he studied it with rising hopes. It wasn't such a bad lie, after all. He was quite lucky, in fact, because it wasn't buried in the rough at all. It had come to rest on a matted patch of greenery and it presented itself clearly to the club.

Now another decision was required. Should he simply get the ball back on the fairway or should he try for the impossible and blast it out onto the green?

From past experience he knew that, if he made a desperate attempt for the green and pulled it off, he would be the instant darling of the gallery. That would compensate for his mistake.

But could he afford the luxury of foolhardiness today? Not in this crucial tournament which would decide his whole golfing future. If he chose caution, he would take a nine iron and sky the ball so that it fell on the fairway directly in front of the green. From there he should be able to sink it in two shots, which would give him his par four for the hole.

On the other hand, if he risked a four iron, he could conceivably put the ball on the green. It might even fall near enough to the hole for him to sink the putt in one. That would give him a three — and a good start to the championship. He would have saved himself from a desperate situation.

Bobby James felt the sweat of indecision. He saw his caddy watching him inscrutably. He had to choose now.

'Four iron,' he said.

Bobby jiggled the club in his hands, but the instrument felt unwieldy. He made a great effort of concentration and swung the club back, bringing it forward with smooth power.

It didn't strike the ball quite as crisply as he would have wished. It travelled about 180 yards in a low trajectory — and scuttled into one of the sand-traps protecting the edge of the green.

Bobby cursed aloud and the caddy looked discreetly away.

On the walk to the sand-trap Bobby assessed his options. He was in trouble now. Really under pressure. He thought to himself, if I blast the ball out of the bunker onto the green and it's not close enough to be sunk in one, I'll have dropped one on par. I *must* get it close to the hole.

He studied the lie of the ball. It wasn't encouraging. Bobby took his sand wedge and carefully calculated the shot.

He needed to take care to hit well behind the ball. In fact, when he finally made the stroke, after much preparation and many false swings, Bobby hit too far behind the ball. It came out of the bunker. It landed on the lip of the green, a good four yards from the hole.

Bobby could have broken the club in frustration and hopeless rage.

Par was impossible now. There was no way he could sink the ball in one from this position. He would have to settle for five, one over par for the hole.

Play safe, he told himself. He had taken a chance in coming out of the rough and look what had happened. Everything had gone wrong. He had to play cautiously and sensibly so that the next putt was a certainty.

As Bobby began to address the ball, a golfing law came into his mind: Never up, never in. In other words, it's better to hit the ball past the hole than not get up close enough.

That thought filled Bobby's mind as he shaped up to the ball. He was so focused on this overpowering need that he quite forgot his ritual twirl of the club. The head of the club smashed against the ball with force and the ball accelerated across the green.

He knew at once that he had hit the ball too hard.

The white globe missed the hole by inches. His directional instinct, about which he had not even thought, had been excellent.

But he'd put too much body into the putt, and the ball came to a halt some three and a half feet beyond the hole. An awkward distance.

Bobby rubbed his hands over his eyes and took a deep breath. He wanted to shout and scream, to vent his sense of impotence and frustration. Instead he walked calmly across the green and took up his stance.

This time the ball would go in and at least he would have the first hole behind him.

He seized the club with clumsy hands and swung it, thinking: I mustn't make the same mistake again, I mustn't over-hit the ball.

The head of the club came neatly against the ball — but only gave it a gentle tap. It rolled slowly towards the hole and trickled to a halt. The ball had travelled four inches!

Bobby was so upset that he felt like hammering the ball into the ground and turning his back on this idiotic game and walking away. But he couldn't — everyone was watching and waiting.

With exaggerated casualness, Bobby took the putter in one hand and flicked the ball towards the hole.

It went wide!

'Why don't you let the others play on, sir?' Bobby heard the soft words of the caddy and he nodded in glum agreement. The caddy waved the others on.

As Bobby and his caddy stood in a silent tableau of depression, the first of his two playing partners took his driver and sent the ball hard and true up the fairway.

The ball landed just in front of the green. The golfer tapped it up to the pin and then sank the putt. He made it look so easy.

The other player followed suit.

Then, his hands shaking, Bobby James laboriously sank the eight-inch putt. He knew that he had put himself out of the contest at the very first hole. Everything had gone wrong. He'd been in the rough and then he'd gone in the bunker. And now he had played like a fumbling amateur going round the course for the first time.

'Bad luck, sir,' said the caddy. Bobby looked at the man, actually seeing him for the first time. 'It happens to us all, doesn't it sir?'

'Yes,' said Bobby.

'I remember watching you three years ago, sir,' said the caddy, his weather-beaten face showing up the laughter lines around his eyes. 'That was one of the most fantastic performances I've ever seen on a golf course, Mr James. You remember — when you single-putted every hole on the course for a sixty-two! That was something to see!'

Bobby James looked at the man again as he smiled and nodded his head in memory of that past triumph.

It was just rubbing salt in the wound. The last thing he needed now was to be reminded of how good he had been — once.

He turned and walked away. He had made up his mind. Golf had betrayed him. The great preoccupation of his life — the sport which had made him a rich man — had now humbled him.

The debacle he had just endured on the golf course would haunt him for the rest of his life. He flushed a dark red at the thought. He got in his car and drove off to his bachelor apartment.

That night Bobby James put the last of the newspapers down and turned on the television to see what final opprobium would be heaped on him in the sports round-up.

The newspapers had varied in their comments. Some had been vicious. One commentator had displayed malicious relish. He had written about the fact that 'even a god of the golf course can prove to have feet of clay'. He had advised his readers not to feel any excess of compassion for Bobby James 'who is probably crying all the way to the bank, when he goes to count the fortune he made from the game before his nerve went'.

Some writers had been kinder, a few had even been compassionate. But each and every one agreed that Bobby James — the golfing phenomenon who had once swept all opposition before him with the reckless assertiveness of his play — was no more. 'A burnt-out case', one man wrote. 'The strain of professional golf has become too great for any but the most exceptional to withstand for more than a few years,' pontificated another.

Bobby looked at the television screen. To his surprise, the programme hardly touched on him at all. The commentator mentioned that Bobby James's game had collapsed in a surprising incident at the first hole, but he went on to add that the vagaries of professional golf were such that James might well be back and playing fine golf in the not too distant future.

This positive remark gave Bobby's spirits a sudden lift, but not for long.

I'm finished, he thought, as he sat alone in his comfortable room.

He knew that he only had to pick up the phone and quite soon the apartment would be full of acquaintances, girlfriends, hangers-on. Warm empty words, easy meaningless flattery — that was no solution.

He raised his hands and looked at them with a kind of wonder.

What had become of the prowess he used to revel in? The ability to swing the club and to *know* — to know for sure — that the ball would travel straight and true to the pin-point position he wanted — to know that the assumption and the fact were identical. That was the most wonderful feeling in the world. All good sportsmen and athletes had that in common. He had discussed it often with others in his field. It was something you either did or didn't have.

He couldn't understand now why his gift had deserted him. What had he done wrong? He wasn't out of condition physically. Unlike many champion golfers he knew, he didn't drink too much, he didn't womanize to any great extent. He had had a physical examination just last month, for the big insurance policy he had taken out for his ex-wife and his child. The doctor had said that he was in tip-top condition, just as he had always been.

Bobby cast his mind back over the months and years.

In the beginning he had been a do-or-die kid. He would lay everything on the line. He would instinctively play the dangerous game rather than the safe and secure one. It had paid off — though he was not sure whether that had been luck or not.

Gradually he had come to realize that there were easier ways of winning — and surer ones.

It was only over the past eighteen months that his game had begun to fade. Slowly at first, then more noticeably — and now disastrously.

His initial drive to the green had begun to go a bit awry — heaven knows why. Everything else seemed to follow from that.

I wonder if I'm having some sort of nervous breakdown? he thought. He'd read somewhere that people in the midst of a breakdown were often the last to suspect it. The thought seemed ridiculous. He was healthy, he ate like a one-man rugby team, and he slept well.

But he knew that golf was a game closely linked to peace of mind. An unhappy mind didn't play a good game of golf. Anyone could tell you that.

Bobby had made a decision that afternoon to leave golf for good.

He didn't need the money — and he could certainly do without the kind of humiliation he had suffered that day.

But he was so much a golfer that he couldn't bring himself to accept the finality of that decision. There had to be another aspect to his dilemma.

Bobby thought back to the doctor he had consulted during the latter stages of his divorce. That was the only time in his life when he had had trouble in getting to sleep. He had gone to see Dr Thomas and he, in turn, had recommended a psychiatrist. Bobby had liked that man.

Far from being a wild-eyed theorist, that particular psychiatrist was an ex-rugby player with a down-to-earth view of life. His help had proved effective and the two men had become friends.

Bobby James picked up the phone impulsively and rang his friend.

After hearing his story, the psychiatrist sent him to see Romark.

Hypnothink in Action

When Bobby James, as I have called him, came to see me, his confidence in his golfing skill had been ground underfoot. His Inner Face was that of a man who had once been a fine golfer but who had deteriorated into a failure.

I persuaded Bobby to explain to me in detail just how his golfing had gone wrong. A clear pattern soon emerged.

When a man has been a weight-lifter for a long time and then, for some reason or other, gives it up, the muscles he has so carefully cultivated lose their reason for existing. So they turn to fat. They lose their efficacy as muscle.

In the case of Bobby James, he had gone to fat — but he had done so mentally.

In the beginning his driving force had been money. He had been hungry for it, as he had said himself. But success had satiated his appetite for money. He had rich pickings on the international golf circuit. He had never been a playboy, so he hadn't squandered his money.

Once the need to make more money had been removed from his consciousness, Bobby began to relax. He lost the killer instinct. He got out of the habit of success. He began to rationalize — to settle for second best. Money wasn't as important as it had once been.

With Bobby, failure was a progressive process. Once he hit the skids, he fell at an accelerating pace.

Now, at this stage in his life, his Inner Face was a mess. But he did have something important going for him — and that was his intense desire to prove everyone wrong and show them all that he was as good a golfer as he had ever been.

I explained the principles of Hypnothink to him and he accepted them readily. I told him that I believed that we could reconstruct his golfing skill and he eagerly agreed to co-operate.

Firstly, I set him a goal to achieve. He would compete in the next major championship — only a few weeks off — and he would win the contest, not merely finish among the leaders. At first he was appalled at the prospect. Humiliation was still fresh in his mind. I insisted, however, that his restoration to what I described as his 'normal' state of golfing prowess would be swifter than he believed possible. And, what was more, that he would use Hypnothink to such effect that he would win by a clear margin.

We began to improve his putting.

Few people among the many thousands of non-golfers who watch the game on television realize just how important putting is in the game. For most golf courses par is seventy-two strokes — four strokes to play each of the eighteen holes. This total includes an allowance of two putts per hole — that is, thirty-six strokes out of the total of seventy-two. If someone playing standard golf three-putts a hole, he loses a shot on par. In the same way, if he one-putts, he gains a shot on par.

The reshaping of Bobby's Inner Face was a rapid process.

We went to a golf course and I placed a number of golf balls four feet from the hole. I asked him to putt the first ball into the hole. He tried — and missed. The ball went slightly to the left. I said nothing, but merely asked him to putt the second ball.

He struck the ball. It went slightly to the right of the hole.

I explained to Bobby that, because he had hit the ball a little to the left the first time, his brain had over-compensated when he played the second shot and that was why he had hit it to the right.

Bobby James had become failure-orientated. The 'normal' thing for him to do was to miss.

I then moved the third ball quite near to the hole and told Bobby that this putt was so easy that even I could sink it.

He hit the ball and it went straight into the hole.

As soon as he sank this putt, I got Bobby to relive the moment, to conjure up in his mind the image of the movement of the club in his hand, the moment of impact between the club-head and the ball, the movement of the ball across the green and its triumphant disappearance into the hole.

I persuaded him to visualize the sequence again and again, until he had the image vividly implanted in his memory cells.

'It was your failure that made you fail,' I told him. 'You slipped into a habit of failure and the habit fed on itself. But now you have a success to feed on. You are now in a success mode.'

I placed the next golf ball further from the hole and told Bobby to visualize the action of striking it with the club.

'You will see into the future,' I told him. You are anticipating a future event. Your club strikes the ball and propels it across the green at precisely the correct speed and in the right direction. It falls into the cup, just as your previous putt did.'

Bobby stood in position for some time, visualizing this sequence of events. Then, mentally relaxed, and with this image uppermost in his mind, he struck the ball. It went straight into the cup.

He turned to me. 'That's the easiest way of putting I've ever come across. It takes all the pressure off.'

He then proceeded to sink all the other balls I had laid out on the green — fourteen of them, one after the other, with hardly a pause between each stroke. He had re-acquired the attitude of success.

The next stage in the reconstruction operation was to re-imbue him with the confident attitude he used to bring to his approach shots.

We had impregnated his Inner Face with a mastery of short putts; now, we had to give him control of the strokes leading up to them.

We concentrated on improving his shot to the green.

We assumed that he had already had a good drive which had fallen within 100 yards of the green. The objective now was to put the ball on the green, near to the cup, for it to be sunk in one putt — and he already *knew* that it was within his power to sink the ball in one.

We positioned ourselves 100 yards from the green. I asked Bobby to cast his mind back to the days when he was playing super-golf — the days when nothing had been impossible — and to remember an occasion when he had had a similar approaching shot to play.

He immediately recalled an almost identical situation — a moment when he had felt such overwhelming confidence that he had believed that the ball was almost certain to roll into the cup — and, in fact, had come tantalizingly close.

I then asked Bobby to make a practice swing with the club, without striking the ball, but visualizing with intense concentration the precise details of the shot which had given him so much pride and satisfaction years before.

I told him that, in his mind's eye, he should see his club strike the ball, feel the jar along his forearms, travelling up to his shoulders, see the flight of the ball through the air, watch it fall on the green and roll towards the pin.

Bobby made numerous practice swings — all the while Hypnothinking his success of a former occasion.

Then, when I thought he was sufficiently prepared, I asked him to approach the actual ball we had placed on the fairway.

It was clear from Bobby's confident relaxed attitude that the Hypnothink process had worked supremely well.

His brain had been programmed in vivid cogent images. Now, as he raised the club and swung it through the air, his brain ensured that the responses of his muscles were precisely those which were required to send the ball hurtling through the air, just as he had visualized it.

The ball fell on the green, just where he wanted it to. And it rolled across the green into an ideal position for putting it into the cup.

'Is that how you envisaged the lie of the ball?' I asked Bobby.

'It is indeed,' he said, impressed and delighted.

'Now,' I pointed out, 'you no longer have to cast your memory into the past for images of success and achievement. You have all the success you need right here — a contemporary accomplishment. Remember this shot when you make another one in a similar situation.'

We went back to the position we had started at and Bobby repeated his success no less than ten times.

Bobby James was playing with the easy efficiency of a computer.

He lifted the club and swung it through the air with a graceful power and the ball rose into the air and soared straight for the green every single time.

Ten golf balls lay on the green — all within a few feet of the pin.

We went to the green and I encouraged Bobby to apply his Hypnothink attitude to the putting process, just as he had done so successfully earlier.

One after another, he putted the ten balls straight into the cup.

Bobby James was positively glowing with the satisfaction of

consistently excellent performance. Frustration and the energy-sapping disappointment of thwarted talent had disappeared from his personality.

I thought that this would be an opportune moment to point out to Bobby that, since we had been on the golf course that day, he had not once displayed the irritating twirl of the club which used to be a characteristic of his playing style.

He looked at me in surprise.

'You're right. But that's amazing! I used to twirl the club every single time I played a stroke. In fact I couldn't play unless I did that first.'

'No longer,' I assured him. 'When you twisted the club in the past, it was an attempt to recreate a remembered situation when you played a superb shot. Your brain linked the twisting movement with the success of the shot. But in the past years the twirling became nothing but a distraction. Now we have dispensed with it for good.'

Our next step was to apply Bobby's newly acquired Hypnothink skill to his drives.

We went back to the tee and I asked him to visualize that each time he drove the ball it would fall at the spot where we had been practising his approach shots to the green.

He spent some time in deep concentration, swinging the club in easy practice strokes as he did so.

Then I placed a real ball on the tee and Bobby lifted the club and swung it — and it connected with precision. The ball lifted into the air and went swooping like a bird to the position he had visualized.

I asked him to continue the practice session until he had repeated this success a dozen times.

Within a few hours Bobby James had regained the prowess which had made him a professional golfer of international status.

A few weeks after our Hypnothink session on the links, Bobby James took part in that tournament — and won it. After that he went to the United States and scored many successes.

I think it is necessary to point out at this stage that Bobby James is a pseudonym. Obviously we do not wish any possible detractors to claim that his success is due to some bizarre hypnotic process.

The truth of the matter is that Hypnothink merely enabled Bobby to remove the psychological blocks which had been allowed to impede his natural talent. He has the superb physical responses of a natural athlete. Without that innate ability he would never have been able to reach the top in the first place — let alone regain the heights from which, for a while, he tumbled.

15.

'Am I the Greatest?'

The huge man seemed a giant among pygmies as he strode along London's Oxford Street, through the dense flow of tourists, shoppers and pedestrians.

He was on his own, which was unusual. His face was set in stern lines — quite unlike his customary expression.

As he moved purposefully, recognition was all around him. His was one of the most internationally known faces in the world. Even as he walked, he noticed the customary responses about him — awe, admiration, sometimes even a tinge of fear as smaller folk scuttled out of his way, looks of appraisal from pretty women, resentment on some male faces.

He was unaffected by it all. Billy Doyle — until recently heavyweight boxing champion of the world — was a worried man.

He was probably the most successful boxer in the history of the world. He had risen from amateur ranks and he had never lost a fight on his way to the world heavyweight crown.

Boxing fans all over the world saw him as a supremely confident man — and an exceptionally articulate one. He demolished his opponents with a flood of invective before he even laid a glove upon them.

But, only a few months earlier, that pattern of success had been interrupted. Billy, utterly confident, had been matched against an opponent whom he regarded with tolerant amusement. Billy had been the odds-on favourite with the bookies and, of course, with the general public.

But Billy Doyle had lost that fight. The other man, Jimmy Baxter, had won through sheer perseverance, courage and superb fitness.

Halfway through the fifth round, Billy Doyle had known that he was going to lose. His legs had begun to fail him — the first time that that had ever happened to him — Doyle, the 'bounding behemoth', as one sportswriter had dubbed him, the only heavyweight who could prance around the ring like a flyweight, his legs like coil-springs of energy.

Billy Doyle had lost. And, because of a technical dispute, the man who had beaten him went on to become official heavyweight champion of the world.

Doyle had obtained a rematch and was due to fight Baxter in a few months time. But, because Baxter had since been beaten by another, Taylor, it would be a non-title match. Taylor was the new champion.

Billy Doyle's present mood was not due to any apprehension about the forthcoming fight against Baxter. He was quite confident that he could take Baxter. But he wasn't sure about Taylor.

Taylor had come from obscurity to become a serious challenger for the world title. In a fluke of timing, he had won his crack at the crown just after Doyle's fiasco of a fight with Baxter.

Now Taylor had just fought a title bout against Baxter — and he had won.

Won was the wrong word, thought Doyle who had just watched a film of the fight in a cinema newsreel. Taylor had pulverized Baxter. He had used him as a chopping block.

If the fight had taken place in Britain where the referees were more humane, the bout would have been stopped long before the final bell. But, in the particular American state where it had been staged, the authorities pandered to the blood-lust of the public — and to the fortune paid by those who watched the fight on cable television.

Billy Doyle was in London to visit an old friend of his — a man who had trained him when he was a raw teenager, and who had become a sort of father-confessor to him.

He was an old man now, and had chosen to settle in Britain where his grandchildren lived. But Doyle respected old Jim McDonald more than anyone he had ever met. And he felt the need to talk to Jim now when, for the first time in years, his resolution seemed shaky and his sense of purpose blurred.

Doyle went back to his expensive hotel where he found his large retinue of aides and hangers-on fretting about his disappearance.

'Where have you been, Billy?' said Luke Thomas, his manager and press agent. 'You can't just go off on your own any more, man. We nearly had the police out looking for you!'

'I had something to do,' grunted Billy. The others knew better than to pursue the subject.

The following day Billy Doyle's car drew up outside the house where old Jim McDonald lived. 'Wait here,' said Billy to the men who had accompanied him. They nodded.

After the greetings and the small talk, Jim took out a bottle of bourbon and put it on the table. He called his wife and she brought a jug of orange juice for Billy.

They began to talk. Slowly the old man coaxed the words from Billy. Like so many men who have a facility for the quick, brilliant phrase, Doyle found it very difficult to speak with honesty about his own problems. It was his custom to fend off enquiries with a swift amusing parry, or a dazzling semi-insult. It was his defence against blows to his ego, just as he defended his body with his quicksilver fists.

But this time it was different. He wanted to tell old Jim what bothered him. He had to ferret out that maggot of worry which was burrowing through his brain and eroding his self-confidence. He didn't quite know how the whole thing had begun. But if anyone in the world could tell him, it was Jim.

The old man, now in his seventies but as sharp as ever, listened for a long time. At last he spoke.

'First of all, Billy, don't kid yourself.' He raised his hand to forestall the boxer's protest. 'We all kid ourselves from time to time.'

'It seems to me that what went wrong was your ego.' He looked at Billy with an old man's twinkle in his eyes. 'You've got the most notorious ego in the world, Billy Doyle, and don't you try and deny it.'

Billy grinned, relaxing back into his heavy chair and enjoying the irreverence with which Jim dealt with him.

'Before your first fight with Baxter, you were riding high — too high. You didn't believe that anyone could ever come along and knock you off your high horse. So what happened? You went and knocked yourself off.'

He poured himself another generous bourbon, tasted it and went on.

'You didn't take Baxter seriously, so you didn't train up to the peak you usually reach for a fight. I could see it on the television clips. You were carrying weight around your middle. You were flabby, man.' He looked at Billy accusingly. 'If I'd been there, I'd have got it off you quick enough. You handed that fight to Baxter. Your legs went, didn't they?'

Billy nodded. 'In the fifth.'

'Thought so,' said the old man. 'You began to back off — and you've never done that before. You gave that fight away — the first time you've been defeated. That must have knocked you right off your perch, eh?' He smiled gently at Billy. He was really fond of that lad.

'What you have to do now is get back in there and beat the hell out of that Baxter. You can do it and you know it.'

'I know that, Jim,' said Billy. 'And I'll train like I never have before. But it isn't Baxter that worries me.'

He paused and was silent for a while — a huge figure slumped in relaxation in front of a white-haired old man.

'I've been doing a lot of thinking lately, Jim,' he said. I know I can take Baxter. But I'm not so sure about Taylor.'

Old Jim said nothing.

'When I lost to Baxter I lost more than just one decision. I lost something much more important — some of my confidence.'

Doyle rose to his feet and stood towering over the old man, his massive hands on his hips.

'How could I let a punk like that steal a decision from under my nose? How could I let myself get that much out of shape? I'm telling you, Jim, I haven't been able to sleep nights since that happened.'

He began to move restlessly around the room, the flow of words spilling out now.

'I went to see the film of the Taylor fight yesterday. He really wiped the floor with Baxter. He really demolished him! He left him a hospital case! When I come up against Baxter for that return fight, he'll be a pushover. Taylor's done the job for me.'

Jim McDonald watched the big man as he paced nervously. Still he said nothing. He just listened.

'You know how old I am, Jim?'

'Sure,' said the old man. 'Thirty-three.'

'Right. And for a boxer that's old. I don't want to wind up with my brains scrambled, throwing a punch whenever an alarm clock goes off. And I'm slowing down. My legs let me down against Baxter.'

'You know the old saying — "They never come back." Well, I've *got* to come back — and against Taylor. I'm worried sick, Jim. And I don't know what to do about it.'

'You just sit down and listen to me now, Billy,' said the old man. His voice was confident and reassuring.

'First of all, you're not too old. That's rubbish. Don't forget that you've practically rewritten the boxing bible. You've broken every rule and superstition in the book. And where did it get you — to the top! You can beat Baxter with one hand behind your back. And you can lick Taylor — though you'll need both hands for him. You know what's wrong with you?' He paused for effect.

Doyle shook his head slowly, his eyes intent on old Jim's gnarled features.

'You're having a confidence crisis, lad. Nothing more, nothing less.'

Doyle was puzzled. He began to speak, but Jim waved him into silence.

'I've seen it happen before. And it usually only happens to the best because they're the ones with enough brains to have imagination. Suddenly something goes wrong — something that makes them think they don't have the old magic any more. And as soon as they begin to think that, they really do begin to slip. Like they say, Billy, it's all in the mind.'

'OK,' said Billy, 'so I admit I'm not as sure of myself as I used to be. What am I going to do about it?'

'I've got an idea,' said Jim. 'You may not like it, but it could work.'

'So what is it?' The younger man was nervous and impatient.

'I think we'll send you to a hypnotist.'

Billy Doyle was appalled.

'A hypnotist! You must be out of your mind.' He raised a big hand in apology.

'Sorry, Jim. I know you mean well. But — a hypnotist! What can a "magic man" like that do for me?'

'This isn't a phoney I want to send you to, Billy. I know this man and he's worked wonders with other boys I've sent to him. He can help you to regain some of your lost confidence, that's all. No miracles — just plain common sense, helped by a little hypnotism.'

Billy Doyle thought for a few seconds. Then his heavy features set into familiar lines of arrogance.

'No, that's out! I don't need a hypnotist — just like I don't need a head-shrinker!'

All his innate egotism had returned. Billy Doyle could accept the need to go a trainer who would discipline his body in preparation for a crucial fight. But he could not conceive of the need to go for what he regarded as treatment for his mind.

He flatly refused. The next day he left London. Two months later he fought Baxter. He won — but it was not a resounding victory by any means. He got the decision on points. All the critics agreed that Billy Doyle had 'slowed down', had 'lost his charisma', had 'failed to show the sort of form that marks a champion'.

One newspaper columnist stated bluntly: 'The man Billy Doyle fought last night was a shambling hulk, a relic of the vicious fighter who defeated Doyle last time. But in spite of this, Doyle only just managed to gain a points decision. I shudder to think of the massacre that will take place when Doyle climbs into the ring against a real killer like Taylor.'

The next day Billy Doyle was back in England, knocking on big Jim McDonald's door.

It was soon afterwards that he met Romark for the first time.

Big Jim McDonald had been introduced to Romark some years previously and was intrigued by his theories. He sent some young boxers along to see Romark for various problems and in each case the results were encouraging. Now, clutching at a straw in his eagerness to help his long-time protégé, he had thought of Romark as the possible source of confidence for Billy Doyle.

As it happened, Doyle consulted Romark just as the theories of Hypnothink were beginning to fall into shape in the hypno-therapist's mind. As a consequence, Doyle became part of an experiment which was much more exciting than Jim McDonald could ever have imagined.

Hypnothink in Action

When McDonald sent Billy Doyle to see me, I realized at once that a unique opportunity had presented itself. Doyle was no pugilistic caricature — a sluggard dulled by brutal punishment in the ring. He was a bright man with a quick brain and a great awareness.

I explained Hypnothink to him and suggested that the application of this new technique could prove far more rewarding than the mere inculcation of confidence through conventional hypnosis.

He agreed at once. Hypnothink struck a chord within him immediately. In fact, he recalled how, when he was 'unbeatable' (as he put it), he used to go to sleep at night while indulging in languid day-dreams about his next fight, during which he would visualize the exact manner of defeat he would inflict upon his opponent.

Doyle was so excited by the prospect of Hypnothink that he suggested that I take over the entire strategy of his training programme for his big fight against Taylor. After consulting with Jim McDonald, I agreed.

As the first step in our Hypnothink reconstruction of Billy Doyle into an invincible boxer, we acquired every available film of the new world champion in action. Some of it was scrappy — just a few fleeting frames from old television coverage, for instance — but all of it was used. We spliced together a healthy amount of footage.

We made Billy Doyle watch that film again and again.

At first the effect was intimidating because Taylor was, without doubt, a superb boxer, a master of ring-craft and an extremely tough individual.

After hours of watching the film, Doyle felt that he knew his future opponent as well as it was possible to know him without actually spending a long time in the ring with him.

Then I asked Billy to evaluate Taylor.'

'Be absolutely realistic,' I told him. 'If anything, overestimate him as an opponent. Make a list of every quality which you regard as an asset in the man. Also, make a list of his weaknesses. Then make a list of your own strong points and defects, including the fact that you are some years older than he is. Be absolutely honest.'

Billy Doyle spent an entire day preparing his list of pros and cons. Proudly he announced that he had done as I requested.

I then asked him to work out a filmscript of a fight between him and Taylor.

'Don't write it down, just plot the script in your mind,' I said. 'Go through it round by round. And don't ever allow either of you to box in a way which you truly believe to be anything other than feasible, knowing your respective limitations.'

Doyle spent another day on this task.

Finally I asked him to spell out his conclusions.

Billy Doyle proved an admirable pupil. The challenge I had set him brought forth a conscientious response. He had prepared a detailed script which resulted in his knocking Taylor out in the eighth round.

Doyle told me that he predicated his entire strategy on something he had observed while watching the film. Taylor was inclined to drop his right whenever he led with his left. This was a potential weakness — a crack in the famed Taylor defence.

Doyle's own tactics would consist of an onslaught on this possible avenue of access to Taylor's vulnerable spot — the area around his eyes.

'If I can keep it up for six or seven rounds, I should be able to go in for the kill in the eighth,' said Billy.

Old Jim, Doyle's other handlers and and I were agreed that there seemed to be sense and logic in the script. So we put it into action . . .

If an observer from Taylor's camp had been able to infiltrate a spy into our quarters, they would have confidently reported that Billy Doyle had taken leave of his senses, judging by what the uninformed would have seen.

Doyle, seated in an armchair in front of his training ring, closed his eyes in thought. Old Jim, watching the clock rang a bell to mark the commencement of the first round.

Silence prevailed as Billy Doyle went off into the world of his imagination, picturing the scenario of his fight with Taylor, going through it in fine detail, punch by punch, movement by movement.

At the end of three minutes, Jim rang the bell again to signify the actual passage of time. There was the customary interval — then the bell was rung again.

This strange routine was followed every day with seriousness — although at first we had to contend with the ignorant amusement of some members of the camp. But they soon fell into line when they realized that Billy Doyle was quite serious about it.

Jim McDonald did not ring a bell to mark the end of round eight. According to Doyle's script, he would win the fight before the end of that round.

Apart from this daily procedure, Doyle was encouraged to programme himself every night before going to sleep. This was no hardship to him, as he had followed this procedure, to some extent, by instinct in earlier days. Now, of course, it was a precision process.

Naturally we did not confine ourselves to mental discipline only

Doyle followed a most strenuous physical programme.

During his sessions with a punchbag, I told him to imagine that the punchbag was actually Taylor. We even put a photograph of Taylor on the punchbag to intensify the conception.

Every time Doyle hit that bag, he believed that he was striking Taylor.

In his track work, Doyle imagined that he was running along with Taylor, who gradually began to drop back due to his inability to keep up with him. Finally, Taylor dropped out altogether.

The emphasis throughout was on Billy Doyle's physical superiority in every aspect of the training sessions.

In the final stages of the training period, we put Doyle in the ring and told him to shadow-box his scenario while Jim rang the bell to signify the times.

It was fascinating to note that, at this stage, Doyle had become so attuned to the Hypnothink process that after exactly three minutes he would stop the shadow-boxing and return to his corner. No bells were rung to warn him of the time. His mental clock had become exact.

In the days just before the fight, Billy Doyle showed his old form when dealing with the media. He announced confidently that he would keep Taylor at it until the eighth round and would then move in and flatten him.

That is precisely what happened.

After two minutes of the eighth round, Doyle was awarded the decision on a TKO. Taylor's eye was bleeding so badly that the referee stopped the fight.

Billy Doyle had come back from the brink of psychological defeat to regain his crown.

But, as I have said, Doyle was an intelligent man. He defended his title one more time and then retired from the ring — with his bank balance bulging and his health intact.

16.

Helping You to Help Yourself with Hypnothink

You may not be a boxer, a golfer or have an obsession with moving furniture around, but the person is rare indeed who does not have the desire to improve his or her life in some way. And now you can do it — you can lose weight, overcome your fears, achieve your goals. All you need is to want the end result sufficiently and to put the principles of Hypnothink into action.

When applying those principles of Hypnothink, beware of negative failure feelings. These emanate from your mind, not from some supernatural source, so you are quite entitled to dismiss them.

Several people, when applying Hypnothink for the first time, were troubled to find that negative thoughts kept intruding when they tried to programme themselves positively.

For example, one agoraphobic (someone who has a fear of open spaces) would visualize himself taking his granddaughter for a walk in the park — a thing he had never been able to do.

Everything would proceed well until, in his mind's eye, he saw the little girl begin to cry, thus forcing him to come back to the safety of his house.

This was just his own mind playing a trick upon him. The mind is an exceedingly tricky customer. The agoraphobiac did not want to venture into an open space, even in his mind's eye, so he invented a situation which would force him to return. What he had to learn to do — and eventually did successfully — was to see himself, in his imagination, continuing on his walk with his little granddaughter until she stopped crying and became her usual happy self.

Never give in to these negative influences. They can always be overcome. We always explain to our patients that, by giving in to these 'negatives', they are displaying a lack of confidence in their own capabilities. You must be aggressive towards negative feelings. Think of them as a challenge to be overcome. Aggression, properly channelled, can be a source of additional strength. Passivity gives us nothing.

Negative feelings need not be liabilities. For instance, when a soccer team plays at home, the vocal support of its followers is an extremely potent force. In an away match, however, the team would confront the exact opposite — noisy hostility. By reacting aggressively to this hostility, however, the team could spur themselves to even greater efforts. They could turn a negative influence to their own advantage and extract a positive result from it.

Every one of us has this personal gremlin which seems to delight in popping negative thoughts into the mainstream of our thinking. To return to the patient suffering from agoraphobia, we told him that, if he couldn't *not think* the negative thought, he should *outwit* it with a *positive* one.

When he sat down and began to programme his thinking, he duly took his granddaughter for a walk to the park. As they were walking along, the little girl began to cry — he could not stop that thought coming into his head. But, instead of simply admitting defeat and bringing her home again, he walked her past the house of one of her little friends. This little girl was playing in the front garden and came over to see her friend. Our patient's granddaughter was soon laughing again and he set off back to the park with both little girls.

So, with resourceful thinking, this man was able to bring himself to the open spaces of the park in his mind's eye. The thought is father to the deed and it wasn't long before he was able physically to transport himself and his granddaughter to the park.

If you make it a habit to fill your mind with positive, desirable images, the negatives will eventually evaporate. In a way, you will be obeying the biblical injunction to overcome evil with good.

Worrying is a bad habit to get into. So many people practise worry until they are expert at it. They think about things which have gone wrong in the past and begin to apply those unpleasant memories and attitudes to the future. What they don't realize is that, by indulging in negative imagery from the past, they are creating a negative future. To make matters worse, the chronic worrier then tries to make a conscious effort to 'stop worrying'. Of course this doesn't work — it merely creates additional tensions. And tensions generate a worry-atmosphere.

What is the solution? The answer is to substitute pleasant,

wholesome images in the Inner Face. These will overwhelm and erase the negatives — the worry images. Go a stage further and create an attitude of mind in which, whenever a negative image occurs, it triggers a good image which contributes to a positive state of mind. Use your negative images as a response stimulator.

This is much easier than you think.

Your brain can be compared to a tape recorder with some good stories with happy endings and some sad stories with unhappy endings. The brain is made up of tens of thousands of ingredients from your past experience. You can juggle these ingredients as you wish. Remember, a broadcasting company edits its tapes. So can you. Cut out the bits you don't like, change the plot, add some extra bits, make yourself the hero! There is no limit to the imagery you can choose. Do what you like!

In his twin books, *The Sins of the Fathers* and *The Curse of the Children,* Romark uses dramatized case histories to show that people are captives of their own childhood — shaped by their parents, who often condemn them to lives of unhappiness. Think how superbly Hypnothink fits into that concept.

In those books, Romark showed how your past influences your present. Hypnothink offers freedom from the past. With Hypnothink, you can make the present influence the past. We are no longer tied down by our character, formed during childhood. In terms of the Hypnothink concept, our characters are changeable, modifiable — even replaceable.

Contemporary psychology tends to hold extremely pessimistic theories — for instance, that most people are bent on self-destruction in one form or another.

Hypnothink liberates us from these self-imposed shackles. It gives us access to true human dignity — which means there is no longer any need to be a helpless victim of bad circumstances. You can assume the responsibility for your own future. You can cope with the past, conquer the present and plan the future.

There is an undoubted link between one's state of mind — or attitude to life — and one's state of body — or physical condition.

Modern medicine believes increasingly in therapies which stimulate the body's own defence mechanism to overcome physical problems. But there is a mysterious power which flows through all of us — a Life Force. Great men in medicine and philosophy recognize its existence, but differ in their definition of it. Freud called it Drive; Jung called it Libido; Janet has termed it Mental Energy. Without being flippant, just think of it as the state of Feeling Good. And the more you have of this Whatever-it-is, the more resistant you are to disease and the younger you will feel. Even physical injuries, such as scratches and cuts, will heal more quickly.

The state of Feeling Good is the opposite of the state of mind mentioned earlier, in which gloom predominates and the mood is down instead of up.

Just as a positive attitude can have a direct organic effect on the body, so is a negative state of mind a liability — and perhaps much more.

Research conducted at the University of Rochester's Medical Centre in New York explored the mental states of forty patients who were about to undergo clinical tests to establish whether or not they had cancer.

Of those forty, fourteen patients confessed to 'feelings of hopelessness'. Twenty-six of the patients said they did not have these feelings of hopelessness.

Of the fourteen who had felt hopeless, no fewer than nine proved to have cancer. Of the twenty-six who did not feel hopeless, only three had cancer.

Dr A. H. Schmale, the physician connected with the research, is on record as observing that 'the subconscious awareness of a malignant growth is within the realms of possibility'.

The psychosomatic link has been established conclusively by Dr Samuel Silverman, the American psychoanalyst. After thirty years of research, he believes that all illnesses are probably the result of interaction between the emotions and the body.

Dr Silverman, Associate Professor of Psychiatry at the Harvard Medical School, noticed while he was analysing patients that dreams, fears and personal associations sometimes prefigured physical diseases.

One woman produced a whole range of thoughts and hints — including a dream in which she rode in a red car with a German shepherd dog. The woman, soon afterwards, developed a case of German measles — the symptom of which is a red rash.

An even more astonishing example of this potent mind-body link was provided by a guilt-ridden professor. This man had a bad sexual relationship with his wife. He also hated his father — to the extent that he actively wished for his death. His father had serious problems with his eyesight.

In flight from his domestic sexual problems, the professor became a voyeur, reading pornography and watching sex exhibitions.

Dr Silverman reports that the burden of guilt created by these associations resulted in the professor developing critical eyesight problems. As a result of detached retinas, he became quite blind.

In four cases reported in his book, *Psychological Clues in Forecasting Physical Illness,* Dr Silverman successfully predicted just when, after severe prolonged stress, illness would come — and which part of the body would suffer.

One successful prediction of imminent respiratory disease came after a patient said that his girlfriend's heavy smoking reminded him of his mother, who had died of a chronic respiratory ailment.

Another clue was that he had dreamed of a nearly forgotten girlfriend and casually mentioned chest pains he had once suffered when involved in a car accident with her.

Dr Silverman asserts that the answer to the question of whether illness is emotionally caused is that it is caused by the interaction of the two.

'The clues are psychological as well as physical,' he says.

When a person develops critical stress and cannot cope, either the mind or the body has to break down. And, should it be a physical illness which strikes, it doesn't do so at random, but at vulnerable spots unique for each of us.

Dr Silverman's research is yet another convincing testimony from modern science that the mind makes the man.

Hypnothink enables each and every one of us to adjust and control our attitude of mind so that we maintain the positive, harmonious outlook which lets us function at our best, both mentally and physically.

It is this attitude of mind which can actually be greatly effective in speeding up the physical healing process.

One of our patients, a man in his early forties, was taken into hospital suffering from acute appendicitis. The operation to remove his appendix was performed on a Tuesday. When he asked how long he was likely to be confined to bed, he was told that the usual period was about a week. He was very anxious about a vital appointment some hundred or so miles away on the Thursday and eventually he persuaded the doctor to allow him to leave the hospital on the Wednesday evening. He drove the hundred miles, kept his appointment, drove back to the hospital and eventually had the stitches removed on the Friday — when he was discharged by his doctor, and pronounced fully recovered.

This attitude of determination is enormously beneficial. The desire to get back to work from a sick bed — or merely to get away from the hospital environment — can provide a powerful inducement which actually speeds the healing process.

An oblique testimony to the effectiveness of the right kind of thinking is provided by the use of placebos by medical men. A placebo, of course, is a harmless substitute passed off by the doctor as an effective medicine. Doctors use them when working with a control group. Nine patients will receive, for example, a new vaccine. The tenth will receive a placebo — not suspecting that it is actually a neutral substance.

It is an established medical fact that placebos often work. The patient thinks and believes that he has been given a valid and effective medicine. The result is that his condition improves. Medical men tend to dismiss the effect of placebos as 'suggestion', but this is not really an explanation. A placebo works because it arouses the expectation of improvement in the mind of the patient — the fact of future good health is created in the mind.

A truly classic example of this sort of situation occurred in a mental hospital in north-west England — where patients were accidentally treated for two years with an electro-convulsive therapy machine which did not work. Nobody noticed — neither the patients nor the medical staff.

This amazing situation was disclosed when the anaesthetist who administered the electro-convulsive therapy (known as ECT) described the episode in a pseudonymous article in *World Medicine* in 1974.

He observed that patients seemed to benefit just as much from being put to sleep in preparation for the treatment as other patients did from the treatment itself.

This strangely effective 'non-ECT' — as the anaesthetist called it — began when a new ECT machine arrived at the hospital to replace the old-fashioned equipment.

'It had dials and lights and switches for different wave forms,' he wrote. 'We started treatment. The patient did not twitch, although the red light went on the the needle moved.'

"Isn't it working?" I said.

"Yes, it is," said the nurse. This sort doesn't give any reaction — it's in the instructions."

The anaesthetist said that that apparatus was used for two years with no complaints.

He wrote: 'Although I did not actually see any consultants, apparently they were satisfied with my work.'

Then a new charge nurse came from another hospital where they had a similar machine. He said that it was not working because the patients were not twitching as they should — presumably as a normal reaction to the sudden flow of electrical current through their bodies.

When the anaesthetist looked into the matter, he found that the machine was indeed not working. All that his patients had been getting for the past two years was a shot of anaesthetic which put them to sleep!

Romark can give you an astonishing example of the power of thought from his own records:

One day I was approached in the street by a man whose face was covered with enormous warts. 'Please help me,' he said. 'I believe you can cure warts.' I looked him full in the eyes and said with all the authority I could muster: 'Your warts will all disappear — there won't be one left by tomorrow morning.' And I walked away.

The next morning that man arrived at my rooms. 'It's a miracle,' he said. His warts had vanished overnight.

It was no miracle. That man believed in my ability to remove warts. He had been impressed by the confidence with which I spoke to him and during the night his brain had made the necessary physical adjustment to accord with his confident expectations. When he woke up, the warts were gone.

Hypnothink can affect the ageing process too. You are as old as you feel — that is not just a meaningless cliché. The generally accepted attitude nowadays is that middle age is the period between thirty-five and fifty-five. Much younger people are inclined to write off anyone over thirty. This is a deplorable negative — and inaccurate — attitude. How much more desirable it would be — and how much more beneficial to the human race — if the public concept of 'middle age' were to change to incorporate the period from seventy upwards.

As one young fifty-year-old woman who was well used to the principles of Hypnothink put it: 'Middle-aged people are those who are at least ten years older than I am.'

It is amazing how many people automatically give themselves a life expectancy equivalent to that of their parents. A great many anxiety neuroses arise from a fear of death which is based on the knowledge that the sufferer is reaching the age at which his or her parents died. It is quite an unfounded fear, of course.

In John Schlindler's admirable book, *How to Live 365 Days a Year* (Prentice-Hall), he enumerates the needs of each human being as being: love, security, creative experience, recognition, new experiences and self-esteem.

We should add one more to that admirable list: The need to be able to look forward to the future with happy anticipation.

One must have somewhere to go.

There are countless examples of people who retire at sixty and are dead by sixty-one. Others keep on working and remain active into their nineties.

Goethe was over eighty when he wrote *Faust*. Edison was still active in his nineties. Picasso was still painting well when he was eighty. The great British actress, Dame Edith Evans, was doing an arduous one-woman show when in her eighties. A. E. Matthews was acting in the West End of London when he died — well into his nineties.

Of course, your mental attitude can have a great effect on your physical appearance. It is very true to say that, if you act and really feel young, you will keep a youthful appearance.

Many married women fall victim to a negative response when they are divorced or widowed. A woman in such a situation can either regard her life as over — and let herself go to seed accordingly — or she can regard the setback as a challenge. If her response is the latter, she will set out to make a new life (and, if she wants it, a new marriage or close relationship) and this setting out will act as a spur and a stimulus. Her personality will blossom, she will look and behave younger. And she will find her new life.

Many people who retire take the attitude that they have not only retired from work, they have retired from life. They tend to describe themselves as 'worn out'. They say that they feel as though they are 'just hanging on'. They have created an Inner Face which shows them as being physically and mentally expended and merely holding on to life with their fingertips. Naturally, the result is that they soon lose that grip on life.

One of the most irritating bits of folklore must be the cliché that 'you can't teach an old dog new tricks'.

This is absolute nonsense. You can!

We have had the most wonderful and satisfying results with elderly patients who are co-operative and prepared to use their imaginations.

Naturally they have a rich and varied stock of experiences on which to draw when using Hypnothink. After all, they have lived for more years.

A man, well into his seventies, was helped to overcome a stammer he had had since the age of three.

Many, many patients in their seventies and eighties have been cured of a wide variety of ailments.

Our goal must be to get more living out of life. To achieve this we must accept whatever wisdom we can derive, whether it comes from science, religion, psychology, or the areas of mysticism.

New knowledge in psychology nearly always comes from non-medical sources. It is only those on the outside who are able to take a truly fresh look at things.

Freud asserted that there must be non-medical psychologists because people who had been trained within that particular discipline tended to propagate the teachings of those from whom they had learned. This would naturally lead to a somewhat restricted view.

Think of some of the world's famous 'outsiders'. Pasteur was not a medical man, yet he invented the process of pasteurization. The Wright brothers, the first men to fly, were bicycle manufacturers. Einstein was a mathematician, not a physicist. Curie was not a qualified doctor.

In experiments conducted with good hypnotic subjects it has been possible to regress them to childhood and even back to the foetal state. Several seemed to go back to previous lives, but this avenue is still very much the subject of exploration and examination. However, there seems to be no doubt that certain powers, presently inexplicable, exist. In a sense, it is these powers that we tap in Hypnothink.

Hypnothink can teach each and every one of us to modify our own personality and to tune in to success and contentment for the rest of our lives.

Epilogue:
Step by Step to Hypnothink

Step 1:   Take the time to sit down and find out what you really think of yourself. What is there in your life that you would like to change? This is a time for sincere self-evaluation — a time to be critical rather than kind.

Step 2:   Learn to relax. This is something over which you must take plenty of time. Practise your relaxation technique over and over again until it becomes second nature to you so that you reach a stage where you can 'switch off' at will.

Step 3:   Once you are sure that you know how to relax, concentrate on building your own 'den' in your mind. Remember to think of that spot at the centre of the wheel — the spot that is always motionless. The den is yours and it is up to you to create the surroundings in which you feel most comfortable. The more you enjoy Hypnothink, the more effective it will be.

Step 4:   Having built your den, set aside a time each day to go into it. Newcomers to Hypnothink often find the 'twilight' time between being awake and falling asleep at night the ideal time to choose. Now decide on your target — just one at a time — and let events happen in your mind. Be specific. See all the details and allow things to take the time they would take in actuality. Really see and feel what is happening. Be involved. Don't just tell yourself what is going on.

Step 5:   Above all — enjoy it! Enjoy the feeling of pleasure and of confidence when you picture your own particular happy ending. Take the time to savour that feeling, knowing that you have earned the right to do so.

Step 6:   Use negative thoughts to help you. Of course it is better if you manage to keep negative thoughts out altogether but, if they should creep in, see them as a challenge and use your own brain to outwit them. Remember the old man who wanted to take his granddaughter to the park. If you can't keep negative thoughts away, turn them to your advantage by making them part of the story.

Step 7:   Repeat the whole process each night before going to sleep. Believe in yourself and in the power of your mind and you cannot fail. Every day practise acting the part of the new person you wish to be. You *are* that person.

Finally, there are a few rules which, if you remember them, will help you along your way.
1. Reach for your target with confidence. Don't entertain a single doubt. You can do anything you want to do.
2. Never feel guilty about being happy. Remember, happiness creates health.
3. Put old hurts and failures behind you. Concentrate only on past successes — no matter how small they may have been.
4. Remember that tightrope-walker and never stagnate. When you have reached your original goal, that's the time to set a new one.
5. Think of negative feelings as a challenge rather than trying to overcome them by force of will.
6. Enjoy every moment of Hypnothink. Enjoy the preparation and the practising. Derive real pleasure from the knowledge that every moment spent working on Hypnothink brings you nearer to being the person you want to be and living the life you want to live.

Index